10678492

MAJORING
in *Your*
MARRIAGE

248.844 W693
Wilson, Frank.
Majoring in your marriage

FRANK & P. BUNNY
WILSON

MID-CONTINENT PUBLIC LIBRARY
Antioch Branch
6060 N. Chestnut Ave.
Gladstone, MO 64119

AN

WITHDRAWN
FROM THE RECORDS OF THE
MID-CONTINENT PUBLIC LIBRARY

HARVEST HOUSE PUBLISHERS

EUGENE, OREGON

Unless otherwise indicated, all Scripture quotations are taken from the HOLY BIBLE, NEW INTERNATIONAL VERSION®. NIV®. Copyright ©1973, 1978, 1984 by the International Bible Society. Used by permission of Zondervan. All rights reserved.

Verses marked KJV are taken from the King James Version of the Bible.

Verses marked NKJV are taken from the New King James Version. Copyright ©1982 by Thomas Nelson, Inc. Used by permission. All rights reserved.

Cover by Koechel Peterson & Associates, Inc., Minneapolis, Minnesota

MAJORING IN YOUR MARRIAGE
Copyright © 1996 by Frank and Bunny Wilson
Published by Harvest House Publishers
Eugene, Oregon 97402
www.harvesthousepublishers.com

Library of Congress Cataloging-in-Publication Data
Wilson, Frank, 1940–
   [Master's degree]
   Majoring in your marriage / Frank & P. Bunny Wilson.
     p. cm.
Originally published: The master's degree. Eugene, Or.: Harvest House, ©1996
   ISBN 0-7369-1366-1 (pbk.)
   1. Spouses—Religious life. 2. Marriage—Religious aspects—Christianity. 3. Wilson, P. B.
(P. Bunny), 1950–   . 4. Wilson, Frank, 1940–   . I. Wilson, P. B. (P. Bunny), 1950– .
II. Title.
   BV4596.M3W57   2004
   248.8'44—dc22   2003021698

All rights reserved. No part of this publication may be reproduced, stored in a retrieval system, or transmitted in any form or by any means—electronic, mechanical, digital, photocopy, recording, or any other—except for brief quotations in printed reviews, without the prior permission of the publisher.

Printed in the United States of America

04 05 06 07 08 09 10 11 / BP / 10 9 8 7 6 5 4 3 2 1

$\mathcal{D}$edication

First, we want to thank God, the Master teacher, for leading us in our marriage from a survivalist mentality to a winning attitude. We dedicate this book to Tom and Jeannine Gonzales, our friends, teachers, and role models who showed us how to pour ourselves into the lives of hurting families and make a difference. We have studied many other good examples of couples who are in the pursuit of excellence for their marriages such as the late Gene Browning and his wife, Shirley; Tony and Lois Evans, Tom (who went home to be with the Lord several years ago) and Barbara Skinner, Cliff and Audree Ashe, and others with whom we have shared this walk.

We thank our children, Tracey, Franco, Launi, Fawn, Christy and Gabrielle, who loaned us to the process of learning biblical principles for developing a godly marriage and family. If any of them were writing this dedication instead of us, they would say we ought to thank them for serving as our guinea pigs while we experimented with a variety of approaches to making our marriage work. In their own way, each one of them has challenged us to a higher level of integrity and purpose for our marriage. We also gained a treasure of wisdom and knowledge from our extraordinary pastor/teacher, the late Dr. E.V. Hill and his dear departed wife, Jane.

$\mathcal{A}$cknowledgments

We wish to thank the following people for their input and critiques: Lela, Meaalofa, Gail, John, Antoinette, Larry, Ginny, Yvonne, Pam, Michael, Charisse, Pat, Warren, Dolores, Frank, Debbie, Keith, Theresa, and Mary. Also a special thank you goes to those friends who provided the means necessary to work on this book: Cliff, Carl, Annette, Jim, Rona, Andrew, Saskia, Saini. We cannot forget the family of talented colaborers at Harvest House Publishers.

Last, but not least, I thank Bunny for not folding under the pressure of relentless assaults against our marriage.

And I thank Frank for pursuing excellence so that our "oneness could be a witness."

MID-CONTINENT PUBLIC LIBRARY

3 0001 01039534 3

MID-CONTINENT PUBLIC LIBRARY
Antioch Branch
6060 N. Chestnut Ave.
Gladstone, MO 64119

AN

Other Books by P.B. Wilson

God Is in the Kitchen Too
God Is in the Bedroom Too
Seven Secrets Women Want to Know
Liberated Through Submission
Knight in Shining Armor

$\mathcal{C}$ontents

$\mathcal{O}$rientation

Bunny

What prepared you for a lifetime commitment to your husband or wife? Were you homeschooled and your parents were your professors? Did you learn through on-the-job training? Wherever you received your training, was it the best place for you to learn the principles of developing an exciting and successful marriage? In far too many cases the answer is a resounding "No!"

Let's look at it from another perspective: Imagine that your marriage is a university and you are going for your Master's Degree. Your spouse is your major. Some of the courses required include communication, romance, sex, finances, in-laws, spiritual maturity, and a foreign language (the unique language spoken by your mate). If you received grades in those subjects today, would they be A's, F's, or something in between? The Lord would be giving the grades with a recommendation from your spouse. With that in mind, what do you think your grade-point average would be?

This book is written to challenge you to go for your M.S.M.—Master's Degree in Successful Marriage. Obtaining an academic master's degree usually takes up to six years of dedicated effort. During that time most men and women face victories and hardships. There are many hours of study and preparation, midterms, and finals. Often there are financial struggles. And, at some point, almost every graduate student asks, "Why am I doing this?" But the rewards of graduating are many and they last a lifetime.

When students have completed their studies, they look forward to graduation day when the mortarboard tassel will be moved from one side to the other, when their friends and family will be hugging and shaking hands with pride, and when they will hear their name called to receive that long-awaited diploma. The gratification may have been delayed, but it was well worth the wait.

Likewise, obtaining the Master's degree in marriage requires that kind of commitment—and more. This honor is earned when you are willing to go to the degree of the Master—Jesus—in your marriage.

We encourage that both marriage partners work through this process together. However, you can work through this book even if your spouse has no interest in participating, because God is working on you alone. Practice being obedient to God's Word, His will and His way apart from the actions of your spouse.

As with any other school in which you enroll, there are guidelines that will guarantee your success. A well-planned course of study will make your learning process easier and more efficient. In the pages that follow, you'll find some important points to remember as you begin traveling the path towards obtaining the Master's degree in Successful Marriage.

Focus Only on *Your* Efforts

At the judgment seat of Christ, when you answer for the works you did on earth, you will stand alone (see Romans 14:10-12). Your husband or wife will not be there. Even if you try to use him or her as an excuse for any ill-behavior, you will more than likely hear from the Father, "Yes, I know what he or she did wrong, but what did I ask *you* to do?"

You may be tempted to highlight portions of this book that point out your spouse's shortcomings. Maybe you'll think about leaving it open to that page so your mate can't miss it. Try not to give in to that temptation! Please don't raise questions about some particular point if your intention is to express your feelings concerning the issue. And, above all, do not say, "I told you so," when you read a portion of material that you have been trying to explain to your spouse for years.

Professors of the Heart

Allow the Holy Spirit to do His work in your spouse. Often we want to play the role of the Holy Spirit in convicting and teaching our spouses. That is not our job. The only thing we are capable of doing is trying to change our spouse's minds. In that regard, a wise person once said,

> A man [or woman] convinced against his will
> Is of the same opinion still.

In areas of growth, your spouse might need a change of heart. This can only be accomplished by Jesus and the Holy Spirit.

It Takes Time

Frank

Obtaining a master's degree can take up to six years. We suggest that you commit a similar amount of time to this Master's degree effort. At first, that may sound like quite a time investment, but *results* take time. Besides, shouldn't we at least give as much concentration to our marriage (in which we promised God and each other "until death do us part") as we do to an earthly education? The truth is, there is no way to judge the condition of our marriages until we do it God's way—and His way takes time.

During those years, you will be planting precious seeds of hope, faith, and love into your marriage. Remember, a tiny acorn develops into a giant oak tree. Your friends and family members will one day be able to sit in the shade of your marriage and realize what happens when people are genuinely committed to each other and to God.

This process, although tremendously rewarding, is not easy. Many of our old negative and destructive patterns have to be destroyed—and those things don't die easily. An accumulation of wrong information may have contributed to your marriage's lack of growth or even its deterioration. That wrong information needs to be replaced with God's wisdom and direction. Only the strong will survive, but whenever you are feeling weak, remember: "I can do all things through Christ which strengtheneth me" (Philippians 4:13 KJV).

Necessary Supplies

Bunny

It is very important for you to do your homework assignments. Some may seem rather simple and basic. However, every successful person, no matter what his or her profession, started with the basics. You will need a notebook to take notes from the book and to complete your homework. You may also use the notebook as a journal. Please strive to complete your assigned work.

It will also be advantageous if you have a prayer partner who is in agreement with this process and is of the same sex as you. It would be best if he or she is also working on this program so you can pray together and be encouraged during the hard times. Don't, however, allow not having such a partner be an excuse for not proceeding with the material. Remember

that Frank and I are praying for you and that we believe in you.
Most of all, God is more than able to aid you.

Assignment

1. Purchase a notebook to complete assignments.

2. Ask God for strength to complete this process.

3. Remember three things you liked about your spouse when
   you first met. Write them down in your notebook.

1

The Power of One

~

Bunny

Throughout this book, Frank and I will interchange thoughts, teachings, and stories. This chapter, however, is special. God has blessed Frank with a complete lesson which shares the tremendous principle of "ONE." He will introduce this very important subject.

We both believe that marriage should be *onederful*! Do you know what it means to be one with your spouse? Perhaps the concept seems too big to grasp. Frank and I once felt that way until the Lord revealed to Frank the power and preciousness of one, and he was able to share that life-changing concept with me.

When we got married, each of us brought a male cat into the marriage—mine was a Siamese and Frank's was a calico. They spent the first several weeks irritating one another until I decided to put them in a room together and announced, "I'm not letting you out until you learn to get along!" They obviously believed me because when they emerged the next day they had become inseparable.

We hope this book will serve the same purpose. We pray it will challenge you to stay together with the goal of working out whatever challenges you're facing in your relationship. By the end, it is our prayer that you, too, will become inseparable in your love and commitment to one another.

One

Frank

As a popular music producer, I watched the combined forces of two or more people blending their talents into the power of "one" to create beautiful music together. Rodgers and Hammerstein, David and Bacharach, and Ashford and Simpson are just a few examples.

I particularly remember one day when a quiet, eerie hush fell across the crowded music company's star-studded meeting room. I was part of a regularly scheduled new product demonstration meeting. One successful producer/writer after another had just heard his recording played before his peers, and each had been enthusiastically applauded.

Now there appeared a brown envelope which contained the latest test recording of a Holland, Dozier and Holland production. As it was passed forward, a sudden, almost reverent quietness charged the surroundings with electricity. Everyone knew that our production team, even though we were new, had recently produced two back-to-back number-one recordings: "Love Child" and "I'm Gonna Make You Love Me." But this team was on a streak of nine straight number-one recordings. They could not miss. They were hot, hot, hot!

Everyone waited breathlessly to hear the tenth straight number-one record/song. At first, the only sound which broke the stillness was the chairman clearing his throat as he gave a nod for the song to be played. Finally, the needle of the turntable touched down on the outer edge of the test copy. Even the surface noise forecast something great. After all, this was the music of Holland, Dozier and Holland, creators of

"Where Did Our Love Go," "Baby Love," "Can't Help Myself,"
"Reach Out," "I Hear a Symphony," and many other recording
masterpieces.

As the music filled the room, no one was disappointed. As
expected, this team had again blended their musical gifts together to create one magnificent universal sound. Their talents had been combined into one source of creative musical
genius. I think I learned one of my early lessons about "oneness" from this experience.

Oneness—From the Beginning

But there is an even more dramatic example of breath-
less anticipation preceding a creative breakthrough. Imagine
what it must have been like during that last instant when
the earth was without form and empty, and darkness was
over the surface of the deep. The Spirit of God was hover-
ing over the waters...and God said, "Let there be light."
Suddenly there was light!

After God had completed the creation of everything in
such magnificent splendor, He "saw that it was good"! But then
a quiet, eerie hush fell ceremoniously across the celestial banis-
ter as a joint declaration was broadcast. Having already wit-
nessed such awesome glory and power, I imagine the angels
waited breathlessly as God prepared to bring forth the crown-
ing achievement of His creation. After all, they had been there,
singing together and shouting for joy, when He'd laid the foundation of the earth. Now as the Creator stoops, He declares:

> Let us make man in our image, after our likeness: and
> let them have dominion...be fruitful, and multiply,
> and replenish the earth, and subdue it (Genesis
> 1:26,28 KJV).

Then, after the creation of male and female, God revealed
His master plan:

A man shall leave his father and his mother, and shall cleave unto his wife: and they shall be *one flesh* (Genesis 2:24 KJV, emphasis added).

The Creator commanded that humans should reflect the image of God by being and acting like the king and queen they were created to be. The man and his wife were both naked, vulnerable, transparent, open before one another, "and they felt no shame." There was no competition, no comparison, no conflict; rather, they celebrated what the Lord had done, coming together emotionally and sexually: They were one. *With the power of His word God made them so.* "God saw all that he had made, and it was very good" (Genesis 1:31).

God's Plan for Oneness

At the very moment Bunny and I realized that the oneness of the husband and wife was divinely ordained at the time of Creation, we became excited. Together, we wanted to experience the maximum potential of that royal decree to be "one flesh," because God Himself said that "it was very good." The only time during creation God said, "it is *not* good" was before the woman was made (see Genesis 2:18). Since God said, "It is not good" for the man to be alone, evidently it was bad. So God completed His plan, making a woman for the man.

Now everything in creation was and is indeed "very good." But perhaps you've wondered what is so good about the unfolding drama of oneness. Of course we know, from a purely humanistic standpoint, that oneness is very valuable. In Genesis 11:6 God says:

If as one people speaking the same language they have begun to do this [build a tower up to heaven], then nothing they plan to do will be impossible for them.

We see additional evidence of this proclamation written across the pages of modern history: the Berlin wall, the Iron Curtain, Poland's Solidarity Movement. We see striking examples of the power of one when we study the ruins of ancient civilizations, such as the Egyptian empires with their giant pyramids, the Roman empire where all roads led to Rome, and the Greek empire whose language blanketed the entire world of its day.

In these societies, people were working together for a common cause. But one fact about them remains perfectly clear: Whatever is built without God as the foundation of human endeavor is destined to someday crumble. Perfect oneness is found only in divinity. The closer humankind comes to oneness with God, the closer they come to oneness with each other. In marriage, when two become one in communion with God, their relationship becomes almost divine.

Oneness Is Practical

The teacher says in Ecclesiastes 4:9, "Two [together] are better than one [alone]" because:

1. They have more profit from their labor.

2. If one falls down, the other person can help him or her up. But pity the person who has no one to help if he falls.

3. If it gets cold, they can warm one another. But how can one alone keep warm?

4. Though one may be overpowered, two can defend themselves. And a three-strand cord is not easily broken.

Jesus says in Luke 11:17, "a house divided against itself will fall." In light of all this, it is obviously wise and practical to stand together as one.

Oneness Is Poetic and Pretty

But there is more. Not only is oneness practical, it is also very picturesque. Have you ever seen a flock of geese flying in tight formation across a cloudless sky or a school of dolphins out for a morning of fun as they frolic together, mimicking the rolling waves of the ocean? Have you observed synchronized swimmers at the Summer Olympics or ice dancers during the international competitions? They move as though each one knows the mind of the other. What classic beauty they exhibit through their oneness!

I also love watching the marines firing their rifles as they salute a fallen comrade at his home-going service. The movements of their white-gloved hands are ordered by force of habit after hours of hearing an often repeated command. Now, with amazing precision, they move together like poetry in motion.

Oneness Is Powerful

Besides beauty, there is power in oneness. Niagara Falls is a good example of this. A nineteenth-century visitor to the Falls wrote, "O what a waste of water power is here! It would move ten thousand water wheels and run them through the year." Later, in 1895, the first large hydraulic turbines were put in place at Niagara to harness all that water through a power-house, providing energy for the entire city of Buffalo, New York. A restless stream of water became a source of power when its energy was brought together for one purpose.

In sports, notice that whenever a talented team learns to think and act as one, they usually win championships. On the other hand, when teams do not function as one because of aggressive egos and internal friction, you may find some great individual records, but there won't be much to celebrate in the win/loss column.

To dramatize the perfect meaning of the power of oneness, we need to look no further than God Himself. The Lord—

Creator of the ends of the earth—is the Father, Son, and the Holy Spirit in One. He is One and we are made in His image.

> And God said, "Let us make man in our image, after our likeness" (Genesis 1:26 KJV).

> That they all may be one; as thou, Father, art in me, and I in thee, that they also may be one in us: that the world may believe that thou hast sent me (John 17:21 KJV).

God did not bring us together to compete against one another but to complement each other and not to be compared to one another but to be companions. God made us to be one.

True Oneness Is the Image of God

How does this work? To be in oneness requires alignment. To be in alignment with another you must also be in agreement. Each year thousands of couples walk together down the aisle of matrimony, but "can two walk together [be in alignment], except they be agreed [be in agreement]?" (Amos 3:3 KJV).

Have you ever driven an automobile that was out of alignment? At times it probably felt like it was coming apart. Until that automobile is properly repaired, everyone inside is going to be pretty well shaken up: husband, wife and children. How many marriages today are like cars out of alignment? How did they get that way? Couples that are out of alignment with the Word of God are out of alignment with each other.

Before Bunny and I could achieve oneness, we had to decide to trust God's Word in directing our relationship or our dream of marriage would have become a frustrating nightmare for both of us. Not being in alignment with each other contributes to confusion about roles, to fear of speaking honestly about what is on your mind, and to frustrating discussions that are seldom, if ever, resolved. Secrets, criticism, and suspicions increase as the relationship struggles to remain intact.

But there is an alternative. Look what happens when you do decide to bring your relationship into alignment, to begin operating as one. Jesus says in Matthew 18:18:

> I tell you the truth, whatever you bind on earth will be bound in heaven, and whatever you loose on earth will be loosed in heaven.

Shall I quote the rest for you? I am glad you asked.

> Again, I tell you that if two of you on earth agree about anything you ask for, it will be done for you by my Father in heaven. For where two or three come together in my name, there am I with them (Matthew 18:19,20).

Bunny and I no longer reach for the telephone to find someone we can agree with in prayer. Instead, we simply grab one another by the hand. When two people pray together as one, there is power enough to solve any problem, resolve any conflict, or overcome any difficulty.

For this principle to be operative, however, Jesus says we must be gathered together *in His name*. We must pray according to His revealed will and character. Harmony with Him causes us to be in harmony with each other because He will be in union with us. What a plan!

Many times in church services we hear sermons on Acts 2 and the day of pentecost. I have heard much emphasis placed on the sound "as of a rushing mighty wind" (KJV); the cloven tongues of fire; the speaking in unlearned languages. But what is often understated is the fact that those 120 disciples of Jesus were *gathered together in one place with one accord*, and the power of God fell upon them all.

In a similar sense, when Christian couples live, think, and speak God's Word within their relationships, God is glorified and His power is manifested through their lives.

Is It Too Late?

Someone may say, "Oh, well, it's too late for us. We've already said too many hurtful things, and you can't unsay what has been said. We have done too much wrong towards each other, and you can't undo what's been done. So we're just waiting for the bell to ring, for the fight to end, for the time to expire on our marriage. Oneness is a dream we may have had once, but it's too late now."

I have heard these words again and again. But I have also discovered that *God specializes in doing the impossible.* If your problem is no greater than Jesus being dead, and if the answer you need is no more challenging than the resurrection, I know there is a miracle waiting for you. Let me explain what I mean.

Put It in God's Hands

During the early years of our marriage, Bunny and I often ate out. In those days, Bunny was just learning to cook. I worked long hours while Bunny managed the home front. Occasionally, I would casually mention to Bunny that I love white navy beans. I mean I like lobster, baked potatoes, grilled fish, and artichoke. But I l-o-v-e navy beans!

Well, after 12 years of marriage, it sank in. Early one afternoon, with my desk filled with unfinished assignments, my phone rang.

"Hi, honey, guess what I made you today."

"What?"

"I made you some navy beans!" Bunny purred.

Needless to say, I was beside myself. I was in complete ecstasy. I sat at my desk for a while with my taste buds poppin' and my mouth watering until I could no longer endure the suspense. I closed down my office in the middle of the day, jumped into my car, and headed for home. I rushed into the house through the breakfast room entry which, coincidentally, is right next to the kitchen.

A strange smell met me at the door. I immediately headed towards the stove when Bunny suddenly startled me with a brisk, "Don't touch that pot!" Now you know I touched that pot because that is precisely why I had hurried home. As I removed the lid, my gravest fears were instantly and sadly confirmed. Have you ever built up expectations for something only to be let way down? All that was in the pot on the stove was water.

Meanwhile, at the sink, feverishly toiling with another pot was Bunny. Upon closer observation, I noticed that she was attempting to salvage the remains of some half-burnt-but-still raw, highly anticipated navy beans. Someone might have said, "Well, it is the thought that counts" but for me, on this day, that simply was not enough. Sympathy I did not have, and being understanding was not uppermost on my mind. Navy beans were.

I politely asked Bunny to step aside. I proceeded to scrape the majority of the beans from the top, separating them from the ones which were stuck to the bottom. Because their flavor had been severely bent in an uncharacteristic direction, my task was not only to save them but to elevate them to the highest level of tasteful satisfaction.

I placed them into the pot of water which was waiting on the stove, and sprinkled in a dash of salt and pepper. Due to the strength of the scorched flavor, I needed a much stronger base stock to curve the flavor towards a new and exciting destination (and bury the other). I selected oxtails. Next I added a touch of sugar, basil, and a couple of seasonings which I knew would cause the entire dish to blend together perfectly.

I placed them atop a low flame and said to Bunny, "Let's you and me go and relax in the living room. We'll let this simmer for a while until the gravy gets really thick." Three hours passed by slowly. We made a pan of cornbread. Then finally we lifted the top from the pot of navy beans and served ourselves a heaping helping. They were extraordinary! They were as good as any I had ever cooked before.

In much the same way, a marriage can be burned up or burned out. It can appear to be ruined; it can seem beyond help; it can look as if it is of no value and not worth saving. Yet, if we simply step aside and take that same marriage and put it in the hands of the Lord, He will slowly transform it.

How can we know when we have placed our relationship in the hands of the Lord? When we realize we aren't worried about it even though, at times, it seems that nothing is changing. When we are following His biblical instructions and depending upon Him (to the best of our ability) because He is the head chef. But first we must take our hands off and place them in the hands of the Master. Then we should relax in the living room—not in the worry or complaining room and not in the dying room. Let us go and sit in the classroom of "patience." And when God is finished, it will be far better than the good (at least what we call good) that we might have accomplished if we had kept it under our own supervision.

Living the Dream

When Bunny and I first got married, we loved the spontaneity of going to unfamiliar places on a moment's notice. We enjoyed having friends drop in for dinner and small talk. We often solved most of the problems of the world in one evening over tea, fresh fruit, and cheese. Even more enjoyable were quiet evenings spent at home alone, curled up in front of a warm crackling fire, a blanket drawn across our feet with only our thoughts to keep us company. We loved to dream about our future together, married forever in a sea of blissfulness. Then slowly, almost imperceptibly, dreaming about living was becoming more real than living the dream.

After the first year of marriage, my ten-year-old daughter came to live with us. Bunny and I also began having children. Suddenly the business of living and making a living started to pile up alongside the monthly bills. The dream of marital bliss seemed to ebb into an ocean of cloudy tomorrows. Sharp, painful barbs began to replace common courtesies. Busyness blocked us from tackling the real villains of selfishness, unforgiveness, and ignorance. These and other challenges became daily stars in our full-feature sitcom entitled, "Death of a Dream, Dismantling of a Marriage."

Fortunately, a single week at a Christian family conference changed us and our marriage forever. We realized that if we wanted to live the dream of marital bliss tomorrow, today we must fight the foes of the family, overcome the barriers to friendship, and prevent the divisive attacks against our quest to enjoy oneness in marriage. It would not be easy to achieve because selfishness and neediness already had a head start. Through years of manipulation and self-absorption they had grown crafty and strong.

We came to see that old ways, old habits, and past weaknesses were about to kidnap our marriage and hold it for an unreasonable ransom. We decided not to give in! Once that decision was made, the lesson we learned was the lesson of oneness.

One into One

The secret to a successful marriage is not one plus one equals two. Marriage is one divided by one equals one; one into one equals one. Frank is into Bunny and Bunny is into Frank. How does this equation work in real life? I heard an allegory many years ago which I have never forgotten. The lesson that it communicates is powerful, and it clearly sums up my point.

A man has a near death experience. During the time he is out of his body, his soul goes to a waiting area where he meets with St. Peter, who gives him a tour of what may be his future home. Their first stop is hell.

As they arrive in hell, Peter leads him into a huge crowded hall. In progress is a great banquet. Filling each table is delectable and delicious-looking food of all kinds. Music blares loudly. Angry voices erupt in the air above the party sound. On each frail face is a look of rage and despair, of madness and mockery. Upon close inspection it is clear that each occupant is held in the ghostly grip of starvation. Yet none can die.

"Why," the man asks, "are they angry and starving?"

Peter replies, "If you look closely you will see strapped to each of their arms extremely long-handled forks and spoons. The handles are so long that it is impossible for anyone to maneuver the food into his mouth. That's why food is strewn all over the place, yet no one can eat. Everyone is starving."

Next, St. Peter leads the man into heaven. Exciting, joyous music can be heard dancing around the walls and ceiling. Happy and delightful conversations fill the air. In front of each celebrant is delicious, delectably prepared food—the same cuisine that filled the tables in hell. Strapped to each of the dinner guests' arms are the same extremely long-handled forks and spoons. But here, in heaven, everyone is filled to contentment. Why? *Because each one is feeding the neighbor across from him.*

In hell each occupant was angry and starving because his sole commitment was to feeding himself or herself. In heaven, all of the celebrants were happy and filled to overflowing satisfaction because each one's commitment was to feeding his or her neighbor. In a selfless, life-giving way, they had become one.

Pursuing Oneness

In the beginning, God said, "a man shall leave his father and his mother, and shall cleave unto his wife: and they shall be one flesh" (Genesis 2:24 KJV). Early in our marriage, Bunny and I sometimes wondered aloud, "What is the real meaning of this command? What rich treasure awaits those who dare to unearth its mystery?"

With the Word of God as our guide and His Spirit as our counselor, through sex, communication, and mutual affirmation, we began to explore "one-flesh" and what God himself declares to be "very good." What we have enjoyed from the Lord's table of grace so far has sharply whetted our appetite for His dessert (which usually comes at the end of the meal).

Oh, what a glitch there would be in earth's beauty if a caterpillar never changed into a butterfly. What if the ugly little duckling never became a swan? What if the tiny acorn never grew into a giant oak tree or night never gave birth to the dawn?

What if you and your mate never become one?

One morning during my time of devotion, I remembered that more than 50 percent of all marriages were ending in divorce. I asked, "Lord, why is that?"

He said, "Frank, it is because the stems are being cut before the flower blooms, and the grapes are being picked before they are ripe and sweet." A slice of life's splendor is carelessly surrendered when marriages are not allowed to reach maturity. When they are cut off, they are robbed of their God-given right to experience a most precious gift: a celebration of *one*.

Reaching oneness is not an *overnight journey*, it is an *overlife journey*. And once you've arrived, you will not wonder how you made it over because you will remember every crack and every crevice along the pathway. You will recall every hill and mountain you had to climb. You will think about each river and stream you had to ford. You will not wonder how you made it over, but you may lament the fact that it took you so long. Bunny and I want to assure you that to be one is *one*derful! And, in the pages that follow, we will do all we can to help you reach your destination.

Assignments

1. Make a decision with your spouse to pursue oneness. If your spouse is not willing, you can still stand for oneness in your heart and work towards that goal by working through these principles and doing those things that make for peace.

2. Describe (in written or spoken words) what oneness would look, feel, and be like if you and your spouse were really one.

3. Pencil your spouse's name on your calendar once a week to make sure the two of you schedule time to yourselves. This is especially important when you have small children.

4. Design a graph that helps you visualize your progress toward oneness. Create a new graph each month and be honest as you keep track of your progress.

Pop Quiz

1. What are the three characteristics of oneness?

2. What are some practical ways a couple can approach becoming one?

3. List three reasons why a couple should pray together.

2

$\mathcal{M}$arriage: A
Spiritual Battleground

Frank

The telephone call came at 3 A.M. It was another urgent plea for help from a married couple in trouble. Like the Lone Ranger and Tonto, Bunny and I dressed quickly and made the ten-minute drive to their home, intending to rescue them.

We had no sooner pulled onto the freeway when we got into a heated argument. Bunny said something that infuriated me. I turned to her fuming and shouted, "I ought to bust you in the mouth!" Fortunately, we both knew that would never happen. We arrived at the couple's house. As we stood on the doorstep waiting for the needy couple to open the door, Bunny and I began to pray. And part of our prayer was to rebuke the evil spirits—not the ones on the other side of the door, but the ones we had brought with us!

This was in the early years of our efforts to help other married couples, and we clearly had some things to learn ourselves. We were just discovering that marriage is not a romantic balcony but a spiritual battleground. Even then, I always wondered why our worst arguments usually happened on the way to church, when we were about to speak at a conference, or while we were trying to help hurting marriages.

For a long time we had remained ignorant of the subtleties of a very sly opponent who hates God to the point of insanity. The opponent's name is Satan. Satan detests the marriage union—it is the physical representation of Christ's relationship with His bride, the church (Ephesians 5:25-27). Satan will stop at nothing to undermine and destroy that testimony. Once Bunny and I became aware of this enemy, we decided to fight back. We purposed in our hearts that our "oneness would be a witness." However, fighting that battle took more than desire; it required a plan.

Military-Minded

Bunny

Imagine that you have a four-year-old daughter. Your spouse is out of town, and in the middle of the night you are awakened by your child's screams. After dashing down a pitch-black hallway, you rush into your daughter's room just in time to see the figure of a man attempting to pull her out of a window! What would you do?

If it were my daughter, I can tell you that kidnapper would have a fight on his hands! He might overwhelm me, but to the best of my ability he would not take my child. There is no question that I would give my life for my daughter. You probably feel the same way.

Now I want to challenge you to carry that same line of thinking into the spiritual realm. Many times the prince of darkness, Satan, is attempting to pull our spouse and/or our children into outer darkness. In the process, we unfortunately have a tendency to take many of their shortcomings personally. In fact, as the devil is pulling we might be tempted to help push instead of fight against the forces of wickedness. If we could learn to fight in the spiritual realm as ferociously as we would in the physical realm, there would be many more victories for the kingdom of God!

What keeps us from fighting the spiritual battle properly? One of the main reasons is that Satan is invisible. That may not sound like a fair fight, but it is reality. If we are not looking with our spiritual eyes, our enemy will continue to win victory after victory. When I shifted my anger from Frank or the children to the real culprit and began to war in the spirit, things began to happen. Many times it wasn't a problem with Frank at all—it was my perception of what was taking place.

When we ask Jesus to become our Lord and Savior, we are inducted into the Lord's army. Picture a soldier dropped behind enemy lines with bombs going off all around him. After gathering his parachute, he picks up his gun, sits on a nearby tree stump and declares, "I don't think I want to get involved." Here's the point: It doesn't matter whether or not he wants to be involved—he *is* involved! He's in the army, and that puts him in the war zone. Either he fights or loses by default.

Now suppose God's army has ranks. What would your position be? Perhaps you're a private. A private is a person who has made the decision to ask Jesus into his or her life but constantly needs to be encouraged to read his or her Bible and to attend church.

Maybe you're a sergeant. You go to church and maybe you even pick up a couple of privates along the way, making sure they get there, too. However, the phrase "spiritual warfare" is not in your vocabulary. You feel victorious just getting through the day without too much tension or stress.

You could be a lieutenant. Lieutenants are sincere in their walk and their commitment to Christ. You are faithful in church attendance and know the value of tithing. You understand that you are warring against a powerful opponent, and you desire to be a good soldier.

Some of you may be captains. Captains not only understand that they're in a war, but they carefully study the strengths and weaknesses of the enemy. A captain is committed to personal, daily devotion and spiritual warfare.

But as you go for your Master's degree, I want to challenge you to become a general—reporting directly to God. A general faces the war with courage and victorious focus. He or she not only understands the strengths and weaknesses of the enemy, but can *think* like the enemy.

General Colin Powell only went to the Middle East on two occasions: at the first stages of Desert Shield and at the beginning of Desert Storm. The rest of the time he was in Washington, D.C. What was he doing? He spent the majority of his time trying to think like Saddam Hussein. If he could reason like his adversary, he would know where he was going to attack. History proves that Powell's judgments were sound. He outsmarted the enemy.

As you study the condition of your marriage, where has Satan been attacking? There are usually a couple of areas where he continues to assault us. Can you identify them? Maybe it's in the areas of finances, sex, in-laws, step-children, career goals, or spiritual immaturity. How have you been handling these challenges when they arrive? Has God been getting the victory or is Satan continuously causing tension and stress in your relationship?

Every marriage has its own private wars. One of the devil's greatest tricks is to make us think it's only happening to us. Are you going to continue to allow him to assault your home or will you rise up and fight?

How to Have a Good Fight

It was my habit to appear at my children's school often and unannounced, much to the dismay of my daughters and their teachers. Sometimes I would sit on the playground right before the classes came out for recess. My girls never knew when they would look up and see me.

One day my eldest daughter, Launi, came home from her fourth grade class and huffed into the kitchen. "Mom!" she said, "I was on the playground today playing with the tether-ball and I swung at the ball and hit this girl in the head by mistake. She hit me three times really hard on my arm. I would have hit her back, but I thought I was going to look up and you would be sitting there!"

Launi continued, "I know I'm a Christian, but Mom—am I supposed to let the kids beat up on me?"

I responded thoughtfully, "No, Launi. The first thing you should do is look around to find a teacher to help you. If there is no adult there, you can defend yourself."

Launi walked out the room shadow-boxing. Over her shoulder, she tossed back the grateful words, "That's all I need to know!"

My daughter was looking for rules on how to have a good fight. If we don't know the rules, we can be knocked out of the possibility of having a successful marriage even before we get started. As Frank often says, "Christians are in a battle, whether they know it or not."

Pound for Pound

Frank

I heard a story about a boxer who was fighting one of his first fights. His trainer had a very positive attitude and worked hard to convey this same attitude to the young boxer. After round one, the boxer came back to his corner with his eyes and face extremely puffy. Not wanting his fighter to succumb to early discouragement, the trainer said, "You're doing great—he hasn't laid a glove on you! Now go and get him!"

Round two was worse than the first round. As the round-ending bell rang, the fighter staggered back to his corner, weary and sore. The trainer threw cool water on him and repeated. "You got him going! You'll take him in the next round. He hasn't laid a glove on you yet!"

As the bell rang for round three, and before the young boxer could get out of his corner, the opponent was all over him, stalking, pounding, and jabbing him. By the time the bell rang, the young boxer hardly had enough strength in his legs to stumble back to the corner. As the battle-weary young warrior slumped onto his stool, the trainer encouraged him further, "This is it! You've got him! You'll knock him out in this round. He hasn't laid a glove on you yet!"

The nearly unconscious and reluctant fighter responded, "Well, if he hasn't laid a glove on me, you'd better keep an eye on the referee because somebody is beating my doggone brains out!"

Sometimes life is like that. You feel like you, your marriage, and your family are being pounded. Yet everyone keeps telling you that you are overreacting: "If you'll just hang in there, you are going to be fine." Pounding us is the enemy's job, but God never intended it to be one sided. First, you need to realize that you are in a fight. Then you can pick up an effective weapon of offense and defense for yourself. Scripture says, "[Take] the sword of the Spirit, which is the word of God" (Ephesians 6:17). So don't quit in your corner; keep fighting for your life. Your opponent may be trained to hurt you, but God is on your side!

The Real War, the Real Enemy

One evening Bunny and I were returning home from an event. The flow of traffic was moderate and Bunny was driving. She and I got into a heated discussion about who said what, why, where, and when. I stated that she had said a certain thing; she argued that she'd never said it. She was upset. I could see that, but it was important to me to make sure I got my point across. I wanted to win!

In that particular conversation, I unwittingly allowed myself to become a pawn of ego and vanity. Bunny and I were in a tragic play and someone else was pulling the strings. In any case, I pressed my argument beyond Bunny's breaking point. She turned, looked at me with daggers in her eyes and yelled,

"You make me sick!" Then she jerked the steering wheel to the right and the car careened into the next lane. What a narrow escape! Fortunately for us, the space in that lane was unoccupied. But much more was at stake than our personal safety.

I could see Bunny had lost control and, in that same instant, I knew this was a defining moment in our marriage. When people say, "You make me sick," they mean they wish you were not there. They wish you would just disappear. I really didn't know what should happen next—I was afraid of what I could say or do. I was trembling. I thank God that I allowed the Holy Spirit to guide me. I responded gently, "Well, you don't make me sick."

Bunny continued, "Well, you make me sick!"

I repeated, "But you don't make me sick."

She reiterated, "Well, you still make me sick!"

That was followed by a deafening silence. Nothing further was said about the incident until a few days later when Bunny told me how embarrassed she was and how the Holy Spirit had chastised her for her behavior. Fortunately, I managed to escape that verbal fray. But I was, as you are, still in the real war.

Bunny

Paul knew the source of the real war. That is why he wrote in Ephesians 6:12 (KJV):

> For we wrestle not against flesh and blood, but against principalitiess, against powers, against the rulers of the darkness of this world, against spiritual wickedness in high places.

Paul was pointing out that the devil would continuously bombard us in the flesh with his thoughts, emotions, and will. In 2 Timothy 4:7 KJV, Paul also says: "I have fought a good fight, I have finished my course, I have kept the faith."

That much-quoted Scripture is recited by Christians desiring to live a victorious life. But the reality is that if Paul had never become a Christian, he could have boldly made the same statement.

Do you remember that Paul's name was Saul before becoming a Christian? (His name was changed after his conversion.) Saul was a very religious man; he was a Pharisee, which was one of the strictest Jewish sects. Saul was so committed to his beliefs that he persecuted Christians—even to the point of watching them being killed. In fact, he obtained an official letter to go to Damascus to hunt down the Christians, whom he deemed an abomination to Judaism.

Saul felt he was commissioned by God to wipe out all Christians. In that light, he could have exclaimed upon his death bed, "I have fought a good fight, I have finished my course, I have kept the faith."

What's most interesting about Paul's statement is that it was made *after* his conversion. And from the time he submitted himself to Jesus Christ there is no recorded incident where he hit anyone (although he was struck many times) or purposefully hurt another person. So the question is, "Who was he fighting?"

Obviously, Paul was fighting the unseen powers of darkness of this world and the weakness of his flesh.

Can This Be Real?

What does all this have to do with marriage? Let me tell you a make-believe yet very true-to-life story that could happen to any couple.

Henry and Sherry had been married for two months when the spirit of Anger overheard them having their first argument.

Anger knocked on their door.

When Sherry answered, Anger was standing there looking kind of haggard. He had just come from next door after visiting Anne who lived there. Anne had turned him away saying, "Anger, you can't come in here. I only have three bedrooms; Peace and Gentleness are in two and me and my husband are in the other. There's no room in this house for you!"

So Anger had come knocking on Sherry's door. As she stood looking at him, he quietly spoke. "Excuse me, ma'am, I don't mean to disturb you. I just happened to overhear you and your husband having an argument and I was just thinking, 'He really doesn't have a right to talk to you like that. After all, he ain't your daddy!'"

Sherry thought about it for a moment and then closed the door. She knew in her heart something was wrong with that statement. Within a few seconds there was a second knock. When she opened the door again Anger spoke quickly, "Excuse me, ma'am, I don't mean any harm but I have a question for you: Do you want him to talk to you like that? If you don't get him straightened out, he's going to do that for the rest of your married life!"

After a brief consideration, Sherry turned, raised her hand, pointed her finger at Henry and shouted, "You have no right to talk to me like that. After all, you ain't my daddy!"

Anger said, "Thank you, ma'am," and slid into the house under Sherry's raised arm. Anger quickly took charge of the household and Henry. He also continued to wear Sherry down with his mental torments. She was so exhausted that one day when Frustration, Doubt, and Fear came knocking, Anger said to Sherry, "Don't get up, honey, I'll answer the door."

Then Sherry attended a weekend Christian women's conference. Afterward, as she pulled into her driveway, Anger looked out the window and shouted, "Hey, Frustration, Doubt, and Fear, get over here! Look at the expression on her face. And what's that she's carrying in her hand? We better get busy."

These troublemakers knew Sherry would come home excited, so they had put a bucket of cold water at the top of the door to cool her off. But, fortunately, Sherry knew what to expect. She stepped out of the way just as the bucket hit the floor. Then she walked over to the wall and with her spiritual hammer and nail, she tacked up a paper that said, "Eviction notice!"

Anger eased up to the note and started to tremble. Frustration pushed him out of the way and said, "Why are you getting so upset? She's just excited because of that women's conference."

Then Anger raised his bony finger and stammered, "Look who signed the thing."

Their eyes went to the bottom of the eviction notice and they said in unison, "In Jesus' name!"

Sherry had learned at the Christian women's conference that her problem was not with her husband. She was wrestling with spiritual wickedness in high places (remember Ephesians 6:12?). When she began to direct her attention to the real culprits, things began to change in her home.

Typically, there are at least five areas vulnerable to attacks against your marriage. Those areas are: communication, money (or lack of it), sex, in-laws, and spiritual immaturity. However, another area of study which we must not overlook is "strongholds in disguise."

Strongholds in Disguise

Frank

Years ago I heard a man say, "When you are dating, you should keep both eyes wide open. Then after you are married, keep them half shut!"

What did he mean? He meant the purpose for dating is to collect data which will assist you in determining the future of a relationship. So often, couples fail to do the most obvious things a person would normally do to try to get to know somebody else.

For instance, if I were interested in purchasing an automobile, I would do far more than kick the tires or take it out for a spin. There are a number of answers I would want before investing a substantial part of my resources. After all, once you have bought it, it's yours.

In a similar sense, after you are married you should no longer be trying to decide whether or not to pursue the relationship. By that time, the question is how to improve your marriage without reflecting a judgmental attitude.

Nevertheless, whether you're dating, engaged, or already married, you are liable to overlook one another's weaknesses. Then, when a problem arises, you'll hear your mate say, "Well, that's just the way I am." You should know, when you hear those words, that it's really another way of announcing that some trait, attitude, or behavior is a *stronghold in disguise*.

During the period of dating, we usually want to make a good impression. We put our best foot forward and drag strongholds behind. What are these strongholds? I call mine *Knarf*. Knarf is Frank spelled backward. He is my twin. He is always with me, but I generally keep him in the background—I especially did so when I was dating. You probably have a twin yourself. So does your spouse. And your twins probably didn't meet until after the wedding.

Let me give you an example. Perhaps while you were dating you met a man or woman who gave every indication that he or she had built his or her whole world around you. Then, after you were ready to make a total commitment, that person suddenly turned ice-cold. What happened? Consider this: A part of him or her was truly delighted to be in a warm and loving relationship. But the person's "twin" remembered the day a parent that had been counted on left—just like that. No more hugs or bed-time stories, no more rolling around on the floor—the parent was just gone. That departing parent took away a sense of security, a feeling of belonging, and a certain assurance that tomorrow will be a happy day.

Psychologists may refer to this twin as hidden or excess baggage. Some people call this twin a "personality trait" or a "bad habit." I call these things "strongholds in disguise." Many times a warm smile hides anger, bitterness, mistrust, or abnormal fears which were created by an abusive or poorly supervised childhood. Sometimes the absence of one or both parents during adolescence causes deep emotional crevices which can only be filled by Christ. You may have to be the one who stands in the gap and prays while your loved one grows spiritually. This period will also reveal the depth of your own spirituality because strongholds in disguise can cause massive disruption in marriages.

We transport patterns from childhood and other relationships, and any pent-up anger, bitterness, or unforgiveness can suddenly be unleashed against a spouse or our children. Dysfunctional family traits, destructive personal habits, and devastating weaknesses can cause the threads of a relationship to slowly unravel unless knots of love are tied at the end of each strand. This is the only way to save the precious marital fabric called "oneness."

Dismantling Strongholds

What is the answer to this dilemma? Bunny and I found it in the power of prayer, which we have chosen to do together as a daily exercise. There is a story in the Bible where Jesus is speaking with his disciples privately about their difficulties in casting out a demon. When one of them asked Him, "Why couldn't we drive it out?" He replied, "This kind can come out only by prayer" (see Mark 9:17-29). In the same way, some mountains will never move except by prayer. Some problems can never be solved except by prayer. Some broken relationships can never be restored except by prayer. Some battles—including marital ones—can never be won except by prayer.

There are other things we can do, but the greatest battles in life are fought and won on our knees. We can try to be nicer, more helpful, more pleasant, or more diligent in relationships, but many things will never change until we pray. And where can you find a more dynamic duo than a married couple that is living and warring together against their common enemies in Jesus' name? When we "pray without ceasing" (I Thessalonians 5:17 KJV)—being in an attitude of prayer—it sets off a spiritual chain reaction which will ultimately catch up with the problem and destroy it.

However, let's not blame Satan for everything. Sometimes the problem is us. Pastor Chuck Singleton says, "Some Christians need to stop spending so much time binding the devil and start binding themselves instead." Oftentimes selfishness will hide its own weaknesses and look for someone else to blame. You probably remember the famous quotation: "Sir, we have found the enemy, and the enemy is *us*."

What can you do when you discover that you are the problem? Take your spouse and/or children by the hand and obey James 5:16:

> Therefore confess your sins to each other and pray for each other so that you may be healed. The prayer of a righteous man is powerful and effective.

Praying together becomes much easier when you realize that you are loved in spite of your weaknesses and shortcomings. I shudder to think of the victories we might have lost: instead, we won because we were able to pray together.

Some of us have items in our emotional closets, attics, and basements, which are holding us back and hindering our growth—things like anger, pride, fear, unforgiveness, jealousy, feelings of being unloved and unappreciated. Let's commit ourselves to clearing all those things out. Clutter in our minds creates clutter in our lives. And with all that excess baggage, trash, and debris around, it's not easy to uncover the culprit—either the enemy our ourselves (or both) who is the real source of the trouble. Satan needs to be located, flushed out, and defeated. And, as Christians, we have the weaponry to defeat him. Let's fight to save our marriages from his relentless attacks.

Assignment

1. Select a daily 10-minute morning time to pray with your spouse (even if it has to be by phone).

2. Earnestly pray for—not at—each other. Remember that prayer is simply talking to God. Sometimes a spouse is very self-conscious about praying with a mate, and maybe he or she has never prayed out loud. Don't be intimidated by those you have heard pray "glorious" prayers. God looks at our hearts.

3. In your notebook, write down and date each prayer request. Later, indicate the date when it is answered. Over the years, this practice will build your faith dramatically.

4. Pray about small things before they become big things.

5. Make a list of some excess baggage many people carry into relationships. Do you see any you are carrying?

6. Mission Impossible: You are being assigned a mission. Should you decide to accept it, it will require you to go deep into enemy territory. No one knows your marriage better than you and your spouse. Your assignment is to put yourself in the enemy's shoes. Picture yourself sitting around Satan's conference table. In front of you is a manila folder with your name and your spouse's name on it. Stamped on the front in bright red letters is: "Destroy!"

    First, it is your job to plot Satan's course of destruction for your marriage. Based on where your relationship is today, what could be its downfall? Where is Satan going to attack? What are his short- and long-range goals to undermine your marriage relationship? You will probably come very close to charting Satan's course because you know your situation intimately.

Second, chart your counterattack as you work through this material. Now get to work!

3

$\mathcal{A}$dvance Communication

$\backsim$

Bunny

As Frank and I drove down the Pasadena Freeway, there was a peaceful, gentle spirit in the car. He looked over at me and whispered softly, "You look beautiful today." I replied, "That's because I'm pampered."

We drove along for another five minutes and then he said in an irritated voice, "What do you mean I'm holding you back? I thought I encouraged you in your pursuits!"

Totally taken aback I asked, "What are you talking about?"

He stated, "I said, 'You look beautiful today,' and you said, 'That's because I'm hampered!'"

I answered, "I didn't say I was *hampered*, I said I was *pampered!*"

We both laughed. Later, reflecting on the conversation, I wondered what would have happened if our level of communication had not grown to where Frank felt the freedom to share his thoughts. Probably a month or so later, in a heated argument, he would have recounted the incident, believing he knew exactly what I had said. By that time, I'm sure nothing could change his mind.

How many times has this happened in your marriage relationship? Do you ever remember saying, "I never said that!" Communication is a developed art. Webster's dictionary says, "It is the art of giving and receiving information." You may give it out, but if it is not being properly or clearly received, you have not really communicated. Our goal is to teach you how to give and receive information accurately and openly.

Vive La Différence!

Frank

Obviously women and men are different. And thank God for the difference! Yes, I am sure you have heard it said that men and women speak different languages. It's true. That is why it is so important for couples to stop and confirm what they think was said in each significant conversation. Sometimes what one thinks was said may not be remotely close to what the other person meant. A careful interpretation is required.

Bunny often remarks that women speak in fine print while men speak in bold print. That is to say that women usually talk in more detail about daily occurrences and their personal feelings than men. This is both a sociological and physiological phenomenon. Women often talk through what they are thinking in order to arrive at their conclusions. A man, on the other hand, may not say very much about a subject until he has carefully evaluated how much needs to be said about it.

There are many differences between how men and women communicate, and it is often a source of much frustration between them. But if we are strongly committed to becoming one, good communication is the key. Just like taking a wrong turn, misunderstandings can be converted into opportunities for seeing views normally missed. But this can only happen if our minds are kept open and our communication maintains a positive flow.

Early in our marriage, Bunny and I were strict vegetarians. That was one of several things which attracted us to each other. Her father is a great guy, but very adept in the art of friendly sarcasm. One day he called for Bunny, and when I answered the telephone, without missing a beat, he said, "Say, Frank, I just finished cutting the lawn. Why don't you come on over for dinner!"

Bunny's sarcasm used to go one step further than her dad's. If she got really upset with me, her verbal slashing would happen so quickly that when she turned and walked out of the room, I would look down and find myself standing in a pool of blood! Of course, she insists that I, too, had my own way of inflicting pain with my dry, dull-knife kind of sarcastic responses and criticism. Not long after we were married, we discovered how words not properly crafted and controlled can be very destructive.

Communication is like nuclear power. It can provide energy for millions of people but it is also very dangerous. Do you remember a few years ago when the United States' president and leaders from other parts of the western world were constantly accusing the Soviet Union of safety violations at the Chernobyl power plant? They asked for authorization to visit the plant and inspect its safeguards against the danger of a nuclear accident.

The Soviet Union refused to cooperate. They claimed that their plant's safeguards were up to standards and posed no real risks to the public. In the meantime, a slow undetected leak had sprung, and before it was discovered hundreds of thousands of people throughout the region were acutely affected or killed by its deadly emissions. Some people are still suffering and dying today because of that disaster. Likewise, in relationships, the tongue has enormous potential for good. But often, when left improperly attended, it can wreak deadly havoc in a hurry.

Words—for Good or for Evil

Proverbs 18:20 suggests we should be careful about the things we say. In order for us to be more precise, it reads: "From the fruit of his mouth a man's stomach is filled; with the harvest from his lips he is satisfied."

This means: "The product of a man's mouth determines the benefit or the detriment he will derive from saying it." To put it more bluntly it states, "If you cannot control your tongue, you will have to live with the consequences." Proverbs 18:6 drives the point home even more: "A fool's lips bring him strife, and his mouth invites a beating."

However, through wisdom we can learn to speak for success. Through wisdom we can learn to say the right thing at the right time. "A wise man's heart guides his mouth, and his lips promote instruction" (Proverbs 16:23).

Words can be a tool or a tomb. They can be a plus or a minus, create dividends or debits, bring a positive return, or reflect a negative balance. Paul advises us in Ephesians 4:29,30:

> Do not let any unwholesome talk come out of your mouths, but only what is helpful for building others up according to their needs, that it may benefit those who listen. And do not grieve the Holy Spirit of God, with whom you were sealed for the day of redemption.

Clearly this Scripture says that it doesn't matter how badly you believe you have to get something "off your chest" or how upset you are or how near to exploding you may be. If your words are not going to build up the listener, if they are not going to minister grace, if they are not likely to generate positive results, don't let them out! Even if you have to swell up like a toad, bite your tongue, or grit your teeth—whatever you must do, do it. But *keep your mouth shut!*

Today, homes are under tremendous attack. Marriages are crumbling; relationships are filled with bitterness. And much of this tragedy is the result of corrupt and unwholesome communication. But you do have a choice. You can order your own world with words. You can contribute to the healthiness of your relationship with the words you choose or refuse.

James 3:5 is very poignant in its warning regarding what can happen when we lose control of the tongue:

> Consider what a great forest is set on fire by a small spark. The tongue also is a fire, a world of evil among the parts of the body. It corrupts the whole person, sets the whole course of his life on fire, and is itself set on fire by hell [the world of condemned beings].

Have you ever heard words coming out of your mouth that shocked even you? At times you may have felt as if there were a little devilish imp sitting on the inside of your ear lobe, egging you on while you were getting your spouse "straightened out." How carelessly we say some things! With reckless abandon, in the heat of an argument, we let it all hang out because we are upset or determined to have things our own way.

After an explosion, we seem to come out of it smelling like the proverbial rose. I say "seem to," because many times a person who has suffered the brunt of another's deadly emotional tirade or insensitive response will simply walk away, holding the pain inside. We may never know the hurts we've caused, the dreams we've shattered, or the emotional downward spirals we've put into motion simply because of our tongues.

Conversations and Consequences

A friend shared a story with me that will forever color how I view conversations with my children. An acquaintance of his was rushing out to keep an appointment. His daughter was trying to get her father's attention in order to share an acute problem she was having. His reply to her was, "I don't have time to talk with you! Can't you see I'm working on something important?" Those words struck like a dagger through her heart. A few weeks later she committed suicide.

We've all heard the playground saying, "Sticks and stones may break my bones but words will never hurt me." That phrase may have a familiar sound, but it is simply not true. *Words kill!* They can kill the spirit of a person. And once the spirit has been killed, the will is weakened and the body is threatened. Unless your words build up another person, don't let them out of your mouth. That is why David, in his prayer to God, says, "Set a guard over my mouth, O LORD; keep watch over the door of my lips" (Psalm 141:3).

The Privilege of Words

Think about it. Of all the creatures in God's creation, only humans have words—and we have millions of them in order to communicate the concepts we hold in our minds. This is true because we are made in the likeness of God. When God speaks, He creates. He articulates His mind. To articulate, according to Webster's dictionary means "to arrange words in an order which presents a clear picture." Man has the privilege and the skill to reflect his likeness to God by communicating a clear picture of his thoughts. Our challenge is to be dedicated enough to our Creator to rise to the level of communication for which we were created. God has set the example: He is so committed to communicating His steadfast love for us that He sent His Word, in the flesh, into the world in order to present to us a clear picture of His love. His Word to us is eternal life.

We have the privilege of sharing God's glory through the use of words. We can reflect God's light in a world that is dark by using the proper words. Words are not mere alphabets strung together upon pieces of paper or carved into tablets of stone. Words are not vowels and consonants but sounds, symbols, and substance which communicate a transcendent reality. Words are vehicles for thoughts and impulses which the mind envisions and then seeks to communicate. We think in pictures but we use words to communicate what we see.

A good example of this concept occurred when I was participating in a relief effort in Africa. In the Semitic language, the word "blessing" is represented by the picture of a camel kneeling and being loaded up with all kinds of goods and supplies. That is the message which excited a group of nomads traveling into Senegal from Mauritania, looking for water during a brutal drought. They were told the name of my team was BARAC (an acronym which described our mission). But in the Semitic language of North Africa and Arabia, "barak" means "a blessing from God." When they heard the word, in their minds they saw the kneeling camel and believed that God was sending a blessing to them.

Think about what pictures your spouse or child may be receiving when you speak to them: affirmation or condemnation, acceptance or rejection, and so on.

The wrong or the careless use of words often communicates the wrong picture. That is one of the reasons why, whenever one spouse threatens divorce, the other spouse sees a picture of a lack of commitment, a lack of trust, a lack of love, or a lack of security in that person. He or she may then begin to envision a response picture which will guard against the impact of being left alone. What was heard by him or her was not d i v-o-i-c-e, but a picture of being left alone and, perhaps, financially devastated and vulnerable. We don't just hear words, we see concepts, ideas, and pictures which can create joy, pain, happiness, love, hurt, acceptance, and forgiveness. With words we have this privilege because we are created in the likeness of God.

The Purpose of Words

The proper use of words serves a specific purpose. Ephesians 4:29 says that we are to use words to build up. We are to create, produce, and promote in ways which will glorify God and reflect His likeness which we bear. Speaking death and not life causes God sorrow: "And do not grieve the Holy Spirit of God, with whom you were sealed for the day of redemption" (Ephesians 4:30).

Words, which are spirit, enable us to have an impact on physical reality. With words we can change a person's situation from despair to hope, from melancholiness to laughter, from doubt to belief. The written or spoken word transports our thoughts. People "see" what you say whether it is true or not.

The Lasting Power of Words

More than 50 years ago, Sir Winston Churchill stood at a podium and delivered perhaps the shortest speech in history to a waiting audience of excited university students. When I see portions of his life portrayed on stage or in films, I can only assume that his speech is indelibly ingrained in the mind of the biographers. I'm sure it was engraved on the minds of those students as well. What did he say? He said three little words three times: "Never give up. Never give up. Never give up!" Then he left the platform.

You've heard the expression: "Let us eat, drink, and be merry for tomorrow we die." This was an Epicurean creed spoken more than 2,000 years ago. Yet today it lives on in the minds of millions as though it were spoken just yesterday. Why? Because words are lasting.

For hundreds of years, people have repeated, "God helps those who help themselves." Perhaps like many others, you thought it was in the Bible. But it is not, and it was a statement made by Benjamin Franklin, and it implies a rather unchristian idea: God, therefore, does not help the helpless. But words are lasting.

Proverbs 18:21 says that words are also powerful because they are life-giving and life-threatening. It says that, "Death and life are in the power of the tongue" (KJV). With words we can give life and with words we can kill. With the simple use of words we can spread a person's popularity or condemn them to obscurity.

Some parents have damaged their children almost beyond repair by reacting to something they've done with "You idiot!" or "That's dumb!" or by tagging them with names such as fatso, dumbo, or pig. You may criticize what your children do, but never criticize who they are. As Dr. Dennis Waitley once said, "Coursing their veins are seeds of greatness, your seed." Therefore, pay attention to what you say and how you say it. According to Proverbs 25:11 (KJV) the right word works: "A word fitly spoken is like apples of gold in pictures of silver." Proverbs 15:23 says the right time waits, while Proverbs 15:28 (NKJV) teaches us that the right way wins.

The Right Way Wins

Jesus gives us the strongest admonition to watch what we say. He says in Matthew 12:36 (KJV):

> But I say unto you, that every idle word that men shall speak, they shall give account thereof in the day of judgment.

Now if that doesn't motivate you to pause and weigh your words, nothing will. It causes me to shift into neutral—*especially when I feel like I have to say something.* Instead of speaking, I try to remember this lesson and then pray this prayer:

> Let the words of my mouth, and the meditation of my heart, be acceptable in thy sight, Oh LORD, my strength, and my redeemer (Psalm 19:14 KJV).

Perhaps before Bunny begins part two of this chapter on advance communication, you would like to bow and pray with me. Stop and remember the times when your mouth was a loose cannon, when you were outraged or trapped, and when you thought a lie or an insult was the only way out. Ask God to forgive you, and agree to ask the one you hurt to forgive you. Then thank God for His forgiveness and for teaching you the power and purity of His kind of communication.

Worlds Apart

Bunny

Frank and I were visiting friends and speaking at a conference in Bermuda. After a long stroll by the ocean, we returned to our room with a rented video player and tape. Nestled in each other's arms, we watched a mystery movie and then decided to go to dinner. As we waited for the appetizer a discussion about the movie ensued. When I mentioned a particular scene that was crucial to uncovering the suspect, Frank said, "That is not what was said at all," and he went on to tell me his idea of the correct statement.

"You have to be kidding!" I responded. "The movie hinged on that statement."

After a vigorous debate and a delicious meal, we returned to the hotel, rented the video player and the movie again and watched it intently to see which one of us had heard correctly. My palms were sweating, my heart rapidly beating as we approached the controversial scene. When the important sentence rolled off the actor's lips, I relaxed in my chair feeling sorry for Frank. My victory was short-lived though, because the second part of the statement was exactly what Frank had remembered. We were both right!

Sometimes a spouse can totally misunderstand what is being spoken (like the confusion over being "pampered" or "hampered"). There are also times, however, when we only hear things in part. And one breakdown in communication can be just as confusing and combustible as another.

Who Taught You How to Communicate?

Communication is the lifeblood of a relationship. No matter what difficulties are faced in marriage, the majority can be worked out with good communication skills. The only problem is that most of us never learned the fine art of communication.

As children we hear the phrase, "Children should be seen and not heard." And, for the most part, our parents did not sit us down on a consistent basis with the intent of teaching us to give and receive information. We were told what to do and we were expected to do it.

When we went to school communication changed. Girls found communication was usually reduced to superficial contacts with perhaps one or two best friends with whom they shared their innermost secrets. And many girls and women can attest to frequent betrayals in those situations.

Meanwhile, boys usually spent extensive time in non-communicative sports where the only thing they heard was the game plan and the grunts that followed. While they played, girls sat in the bleachers and discussed everything from makeup to politics. Is it any wonder males and females communicate differently?

Now, let's look at a faithful couple at their local church. One day the wife becomes ill and is unable to attend. When the husband returns home from the Sunday service she anxiously asks, "How was church?"

"Fine," her husband responds.

"What did the pastor talk about?"

"God."

Now, let's reverse the order. The husband is sick and the wife attends church. After the service, when she walks in the bedroom with a cup of hot tea for her husband, he asks, "How was church?"

"Well, you know I left 15 minutes late. I just knew Mrs. Smith would be in my parking space. Sure enough when I arrived she was just pulling in. She had a hat on that was so big I knew I'd better not sit behind her. It was hot on one side of the church, cold on the other. I was hoping they would sing one of my favorite songs but you know we have that new choir director...."

As you can see, our schools of communication probably have many flaws and, unless you decide to go for your Master's degree in communication, there is a good chance you will repeatedly make destructive mistakes with your spouse. Communication can be like rain dropping on a rock. After a while you look up and the gulf between the two of you is as wide as the Grand Canyon.

Frank and I hope to help you construct a bridge of good communication so that you can freely cross over into each other's feelings and thoughts without fear of being thrown into the chasm below.

First, recognize that you were probably not taught how to effectively communicate while you were growing up and that you need instruction.

Second, take your eyes off your spouse and allow God to focus on teaching you. "A man [or woman] reaps what he sows" (Galatians 6:7), should be your theme Scripture.

Third, recognize that it takes time for plants to grow. You will not learn communication overnight; you will practice it for the rest of your life. Our pastor says, "You can't ripen a peach with a blowtorch!" and that can be properly applied to the art of learning communication. It takes patience and practice to develop good skills.

Let's Exercise

There are two forms of communication: positive and negative. Take out a piece of paper and draw a line down the center. At the top of the page on the left hand side draw a trash can. On the right-hand side quickly draw a bank. Whether to a trash can or to a bank, you are continuously making deposits through your style of communication.

As counselors, we often hear, "My spouse and I just don't communicate." That isn't true. There is never a time when we are not communicating. Communication is not only verbal, it is also nonverbal. It includes facial expressions, gestures, attitudes, and actions. If you're talking to your spouse and he or she walks out of the room, what is that person communicating? If you're talking over dinner in a restaurant and your spouse is looking intently in your eyes, smiling and nodding affirmatively as you speak, what is being communicated? One action is negative, the other positive.

Now, back to your paper. Number the left-side from 1 to 15 (vertically). Now fill in the blanks. List as many negative signs of communication in your marriage that come to mind. Don't list only your spouse's *words,* but also whatever *actions* of his or hers that shuts down communication with you.

Are you done? Now let's make a list on the positive side. Now turn to the last two pages of this chapter and find our lists. How much of your communication lists matched ours? Our goal is to eradicate the negative and practice the positive communication styles.

Now, let's take a closer look at negative and positive communication messages.

Negative–Frowning
Positive–Smiling

The expression on a person's face can stimulate us to continue talking or to shut down. For years I didn't realize that I was frowning when Frank talked. One day he brought it to my attention after I had complimented him on a tremendous sermon he had preached. He replied, "I'm surprised you feel that way, because you frowned through the whole service."

From my standpoint, it was a compliment to Frank. My frowning represented the fact that I was listening intently to what he was saying. But what was it communicating? In Frank's interpretation, my frown caused him to wonder, "What did I say wrong?" and "Is my tie crooked?"

Even today I find myself reaching up and rubbing my forehead just to make sure I am not frowning when Frank is talking. Whenever possible I smile and nod to let him know that I am listening and care about what he has to say.

Negative–Criticism and Comparing
Positive–Edifying

Have you discovered that criticism doesn't work? Why? Because the only thing criticism stimulates is defensive justification. Every human wants to feel loved, accepted, and appreciated. When we are criticized, we instinctively feel that it is of the utmost importance that we defend why we do what we do.

A friend wrote a song lyric that said, "If you build a fence all around me, no one will know when I'm down."

It's important that we learn to build up each other—despite our weaknesses—and to encourage each other in our strengths.

So how should spouses find areas in which they need to grow? When Frank pointed out that I often frowned, he told me the truth in love, not in criticism (see Ephesians 4:15). Beneath his statement was the unmovable fact that he was going to love me whether I stopped frowning or not. His comment was an identification, not a criticism. He was not putting me down; he was simply stating a fact. He was not angry; he was observant. There was no pressure on me to change, and he never brought it up again.

It's also important that our attitude of acceptance and encouragement far outweighs any corrective observations we might make. When I used to tell Frank something that I felt needed correcting, I expected to see a change the next day. I couldn't understand why he just couldn't decide to do things differently. I had to realize that he was dealing with a lifetime of habits, that he had to determine it was important to change in that area, and that it would take time to adjust to a new mindset and pattern of behavior.

Negative–Being Cut Off or Having Someone Walk Out
Positive–Listening and Active Questioning

Cutting your spouse off in the middle of a sentence or walking out of the room while he or she is still talking communicates that you feel what is being said is not important. (After all, you already know what he or she is going to say...) So, if you stop them midway through his or her statement, you can shorten the conversation and get your spouse straightened out at the same time. You can't get much more negative than that!

On the positive side, when we take the time to listen and ask questions about what our spouse is saying, it sends a message that says, "I think what you have to say is important. I'm asking you a question about what you said because I want to know more."

One day I questioned Frank about a decision he had made. (I was not in agreement with him.) Immediately I saw an invisible wall go up around him because he could feel an attack coming. He remembered the days when I would ask a question—not because I wanted to know the answer but because I wanted to give him the answer. I quickly said, "You know, Frank, I am not asking you a question regarding your decision because I want to challenge you. I honestly want to know how you arrived at that choice."

As Frank began to explain the mental steps he took to arrive at his decision, I could clearly understand why he made the choice, even though I still did not agree with him.

Listening skills is the one element of communication that most of us sorely lack. We usually spend most of our time thinking about what we are going to say rather than being genuinely interested in what is being said.

Negative–Correcting in public
Positive–Supportiveness

Not only is it important that your spouse feel you think positively about him or her, it is a tremendous boost for his or her morale when you openly share that compliment with other people.

We, in essence, provide a platform from which our spouses are heard. If people determine that we have very little regard for our spouse's mind or character, they will unconsciously feel the same way without being able to put their finger on the reason.

Negative–Lying, Deceit, Unfaithfulness
Positive–Honesty and Trust

Trust is a vital part of every relationship. When it is broken it takes a devastating toll. Can a marriage be revived when it is violated by an act of untrustworthiness? The answer is yes, but it is not easy.

It's important to understand that trust is earned. When we begin a relationship, it is only fair to start out by giving the other person our trust. In my book *Knight in Shining Armor*, I emphasize that it is important to discover if your potential spouse has a track record of honesty. If he or she is a liar, is deceitful, or is untrustworthy, it will be evident in other relationships, especially with family. You should be particularly observant prior to marriage regarding this terrible flaw.

Once you are married and trust is violated, let your spouse know that he or she will need to earn your trust and be specific about what they need to do to establish it once again. A commitment to honor and integrity is essential to successful marriage.

If you are tempted to be untrustworthy in your relationship, remember the tremendous consequences that will come if you decide to give in. Hopefully, you will have the good sense not to head in the wrong direction.

Negative–"Your Fault" Messages (Blaming)
Positive–"What Can I Do to Help?"

Once again, you probably know that when you blame your spouse for something, he or she will justify the questioned actions. That is why the blame game is futile.

I hope, instead, you'll learn to say the phrase, "I have a problem with..."

You might be thinking, "But that isn't true." Yes it is. You see, when your spouse does something you feel is wrong or irritating, the truth is he or she is causing a problem for you. It may not be a problem for him or her at all. By sharing your challenge with your mate and communicating it clearly, perhaps the love your partner has for you will stimulate him or her to want to make a correction in that area.

When you say, "What can I do to help?" it signals that you are willing to be an active part of the solution. It removes the need of justification from your spouse.

Negative–Forgetting Special Occasions; Unthoughtfulness
Positive–Thoughtfulness and Courtesy

Being thoughtful is very positive to a relationship. In fact, I know some marriages that have ended because a birthday or anniversary was forgotten. I am convinced that if everyday common courtesies were practiced it would make a significant difference in most troubled marriages. Statements like, "Please," "Thank you," "May I," "Can I get you something to drink?" or "Excuse me," are comments we make every day—but not always to our spouses.

Negative–Hitting and Shouting
Positive–Gentle Touching

A man once said to me, "I really love my wife but sometimes she makes me so angry, I just can't help but hit her."

My response to him was, "You could help yourself if it were Mike Tyson."

The truth is, this man calculated the damage that might be done to his person, decided it would be minimal, and so chose to lose his temper. Under other circumstances he would be more than capable of controlling himself.

Many times being out of control is a problem that needs to be corrected through counseling. If you are being abused (I'm speaking to husband or wife), find a safe house and let your spouse know you are not leaving the relationship—you are leaving his or her behavior. Also inform him or her that you are willing to return once he or she has received thorough counseling and the counselor says it is safe for you to go back. That is how we use tough love to help our spouses regain a positive approach to life.

Hitting is clearly negative, but loving touch is positive. Have you ever felt down or discouraged and then someone came up and touched your shoulder or arm? Positive touch says "I'm with you." Sometimes a hug is worth a thousand words.

Negative–Jesting
Positive–Joking

The Bible teaches us that jesting is a sin but joking is not (see Ephesians 5:4 KJV). Jesting is laughter at the expense of another person—and couples do it more often than you might think. By the time a few "zingers" have been exchanged, everyone in the room is laughing—except your spouse.

Proverbs teaches that laughter is good for the soul. A witty saying or funny joke can bring much joy into an individual's life.

Negative–Disregard of Person's Feelings
Positive–Emotional Sensitivity

It's important to remember that how a person feels is, at that moment, their emotional reality. We need to allow our spouses to express how they feel even if we don't understand. Ask the Lord to help you identify with your husband or wife's feelings even if it means searching for a common ground of experience apart from what is presently happening.

Negative–Always and Never
Positive–Don't Make Sweeping Judgments

When we say, "You *always*..." or "You *never*..." in communicating with our spouses it undermines our relationships. The only thing absolute in life is God. A person is not "never" or "always" anything.

If Frank points out to me an area in which I need to grow, and I really apply myself to do better, how destructive do you think it would be if he says, "You never..." and applies it to the very thing I have been striving to change? It would totally negate any efforts I have made, and I might respond with an attitude that says, "If you think I 'never' did it before, just hold your breath until I try to do it again!"

Try to replace "always" or "never" with "seldom" or "hardly." Better yet—don't generalize at all.

The Finish Line

Frank

When will you cross the finish line of good communication? Do you wonder if you will ever arrive? Speaking from our experience, we were married in 1973 and not one day goes by without us practicing the principles outlined in this book. Married couples will never "arrive" as long as we are living on planet Earth, but we can continuously work to perfect our expressions of thoughts, feelings, and ideas. It is a fascinating and challenging journey.

What is your communication story? In what areas do you struggle? Are you content to stay in that place, reaping what you have sown? Or will you choose to communicate God's way? The improvement process may appear to move slowly at first, but as you continue to practice you will notice old habits falling away and a new style of speaking and listening appearing in your life. We hope you'll be inspired to practice with all your might so that you can bring forth "life," not "death," with the power of your words.

Assignment

1. Write or type the positive forms of communication on a piece of paper and post the list on your bathroom mirror or refrigerator. Look at it often and compare your attitudes, words and actions with the list.

2. Begin complimenting your spouse three times a day (even for the little things).

Negative Communication

Frowning

Criticism (even constructive if it's at the wrong time)

Being cut off in the middle of a sentence

Being corrected in public

Lying and deceitfulness

"Your fault" messages (blaming)

Comparing

Forgetting special occasions

No eye contact

Walking out of the room while you are talking

Unfaithfulness

Hitting and shouting

Cruel jesting or mocking

Disregard of your feelings

Discourtesy

Positive Communication

Smiling

Nodding affirmatively as you speak

Eye contact

Touching

Listening

"What can I do to help?" messages

Edifying

Emotional Sensitivity

Body language

"I'm sorry, please forgive me" messages

Forgiveness

Trust

Supportive

Thoughtfulness

Listening and active questioning

4

*L*et's Talk About Sex

Frank

I t wasn't until we wrote this book together that I realized how many "freeway incidents" Bunny and I have experienced together. Maybe we should have chosen the title "On the Road Again!" After reliving most of them, one of those incidents is more unforgettable than all the rest. We had been married only five years, and I can remember the exact exit we were passing on the freeway when Bunny looked at me downcast and said, "I have something to tell you."

I glanced over and said, "OK."

She began to cry, which was very unusual for Bunny. My heart started racing and my skin became clammy. My mind rushed to think what she might be about to say. Was she having an affair? Did she want a divorce?

Finally she sobbed, "I have never been sexually satisfied!"

I didn't know whether to feel relieved or shocked. How could this be? There had been no indication—or had I been totally blind?

Bunny

No, he had not been blind. For five years I had pretended to be sexually satisfied. As a matter of fact, I believe the Academy Awards go to the wrong people every year. An Oscar should be presented to every wife who has convinced her husband that he has taken her to the moon when, in fact, he hasn't gone to the end of the block!

Frank

My deep love for Bunny overwhelmed any other feelings. I purposed in my heart that we would face the problem and solve it. It didn't happen overnight, but our sexual relationship today is one step short of heaven—for *both* of us. This chapter chronicles the discoveries we made along the way to a satisfying sexual life.

Who Taught You About Sex?

Bunny

Where do we learn about sex? From adolescent girlfriends who discussed the subject in whispers. In the locker room where boys were keeping score. Let's not forget the romantic movies or, unfortunately for some, pornographic movies or magazines. Then there were the parents who frowned every time the subject was mentioned. My mother is a lovely woman but she referred to sex as a "duty." I don't know about you, but I was not interested in sexual "duty."

Is it any wonder that there are so many challenges in our marriages when we enter into them with virtually no knowledge about communication or sex? These two matters are essential ingredients to a long, satisfying relationship, yet we are often completely uninformed about either one.

While I was speaking to a group of over 5000 women, I asked, "How many of you had mothers who sat you down as a teenager and said, 'Sex is good! It was intended by God to be fully enjoyed within the boundaries of marriage?'"

Only two women raised their hands.

I then posed the following question, "If you were not taught that sex is good, what are you teaching your children?" The room became unusually silent.

The truth is, we are dealing with generations of misinformation. And it's not just women who are misinformed. Men are deceived also.

A Poor Example

Frank

According to the Bible, the reason marriage is holy and honorable is because it was created and ordained by a holy God. And one of the many activities which define marriage is sex. Therefore, since marriage is holy, sex is also a holy act. On the other hand, sex outside marriage is dishonorable and leads to serious consequences which carry over into the marriage.

Robert, a young man in his twenties, was deep in thought when I interrupted him. I had just finished speaking to a men's group about reconciliation between fathers and sons, and he caught my attention. "What are you thinking?" I inquired.

"I'm thinking about my dad," he replied. "I rarely see him. He travels a lot. When I was growing up, I saw him only if his work brought him through town. We never had father/son discussions. From my earliest remembrance the first question he would always ask with a sly smile when he'd see me was, 'Have you enjoyed a young lady recently?'

"He equated my becoming a man with how regularly I was able to have sex with a girl. So sex was my manhood. Now, even as a grown man, having sex and gaining respect from my father are synonymous. Unfortunately, that is my most vivid memory of my dad. My view of sex is unquestionably distorted and improper—and it's hurting my marriage."

Robert and I began to talk about God's biblical plan for sex. I explained that there are some people who view sex as so holy they seldom, if ever, enjoy it. For them, it is a responsibility exclusively intended to bring children into the world. My answer to that is that if an automobile was exclusively for transportation many features in the car would be unnecessary, such as the radio, air conditioning, and reclining seats.

There are those who are addicted to and fall into all kinds of sexual perversions. Others see sex as so sinful they feel dirty after a satisfying evening. Most women and some men who have been severely abused sexually are understandably emotionally and mentally unable to view sex as pleasurable. Some Christians think the flesh is so depraved that to engage in any pleasure of the flesh is to give Satan a foothold for dragging them back into the world. They, therefore, abstain altogether. Or worse yet, a few of them sneak out at night into red-light districts to be sexually relieved. God never intended for illicit sex to be used as a secret remedy for hypertension!

God's Plan for Sex

Like hunger and appreciation for food, God has, in somewhat the same way, placed abundant seed and sexual desire inside man. God commanded man to be fruitful and multiply—to replenish the earth. But does God really want us to enjoy sex?

One could argue the point that because mankind desires to live on forever through his heritage, creating offspring would be incentive enough for having sex. The truth of the matter is that if sex didn't feel good, by now most children would probably be test-tube babies brought to term through incubation. Even so, however, I don't think God created "feel good" senses or taste buds as a reward for obedience or as an inducement or incentive.

I believe that God gave us "feel good" senses simply as a wonderful blessing because of His loving kindness and abundant goodness. After He created Adam and Eve, Genesis 1:28 says,

"*God blessed them.*" The real reason for our abilities and opportunities to "feel good" is contained in those three words. Therefore, to enjoy sex within the holy state of marriage is a blessing from God. The writer of Hebrews 13:4 states:

> Marriage should be honored by all, and the marriage bed [sex] kept pure, for God will judge the adulterer and all the sexually immoral [including fornicators].

In addition to a beautifully sculptured description of love, the Song of Solomon explores three aspects of sex: the dream, the drive, and the drama. The apex of the sexual act is the dream of every person God has gifted with marriage to honor their marriage with a bed they both enjoy. The drive is the desire which the Shulamite woman and Solomon have for each other. The drama is poured out across countless pages of romantic musings. For instance, listen to the Song of Solomon 7:10-13:

> I belong to my lover, and his desire is for me. Come, my lover, let us go to the countryside, let us spend the night in the villages. Let us go early to the vineyards to see if the vines have budded, if their blossoms have opened, and if the pomegranates are in bloom—there I will give you my love. The mandrakes send out their fragrance, and at our door is every delicacy, both new and old, that I have stored up for you, my lover.

This couple is planning to have a great time, and it sounds like they enjoy one another. Could that mean they have equal desire?

Equal Rights

Bunny

It's clear from the way God designed our bodies that He intends for us to delight in the act of sex. He even gave us the freedom to enjoy it, saying in Proverbs 5:18:

> May your fountain be blessed, and may you rejoice in the wife of your youth. A loving doe, a graceful deer— may her breasts satisfy you always, may you ever be captivated by her love.

Not only do we have the freedom to enjoy sex; God gave us an equal desire for it. Now I know that rocks the teaching we have received that convinces us that women do not have the same sexual desires as men. But I beg to differ. Upon close inspection, I think we will discover that God is, in fact, a just God.

Let's begin with the question, Why would God give us two different levels of sexual desire? To torture us? According to some people, we have a man who has to be tied to a stake with chains to control his sexual desires. Meanwhile, his woman sits idly by waiting for that occasional moment when she is in the mood. That stands in stark contrast to 1 Corinthians 7:3-5 NKJV:

> Let the husband render to his wife the affection due her, and likewise also the wife to her husband. The wife does not have authority over her own body, but the husband does. And likewise the husband does not have authority over his own body, but the wife does. Do not deprive one another except with consent for a time, that you may give yourselves to fasting and prayer; and come together again so that Satan does not tempt you because of your lack of self-control.

All too often we hear the first part of that Scripture recited, stating that the woman should relinquish her body when her husband desires it. Yet the second part of the passage gives the same instruction to the husband concerning his wife's needs. Whenever she sexually desires him, he should submit his body to her. Does that sound like inequality?

Maybe you're about to say, "Fine, but the woman doesn't desire it as much or as often."

Who taught you that? Oh, I know, it's scientific. After all, so much research has gone into asking thousands of women, who are filled with misinformation concerning sex, about their desires. The truth is, until a woman enjoys having sex there is no way for her to determine her level of desire.

Take for example the woman who loves (lives) to shop. When she sees a mall her eyes glaze over. She dreams of 50-percent off the already-reduced price. Let's use "Suzy" as an illustration.

Suzy has been married for ten years. She was taught that sex is a duty. Participating in the act twice a month is more than enough for her. After taking care of the children, the house, and working, she has absolutely no energy to participate in sex. However, Suzy loves to shop.

One Saturday morning Suzy wakes up still exhausted from her long work week. As her husband turns over and places his sleepy arm across her she silently prays, "Oh God, I hope he doesn't want to have sex this morning. I am totally drained."

Just then the phone rings. She picks it up quickly so as not to disturb her husband. "Hi, Suzy!" chirps her friend Pam.

"Why do you sound so happy this morning?" Suzy sleepily asks.

Pam replies, "Because I just went to the mailbox and received a $500 check from my mom. She put in special instructions that read, 'Please share this money with Suzy—she is such a sweetheart. My special instructions are that you and Suzy must spend it on the day you receive it and you must do it at the mall. Love, Mom.'"

Suzy sits straight up in bed and shouts, "You're kidding!" As she throws back the covers and hops out of bed, she asks, "How long will it take you to get here?"

Pam laughs, "I'm on my way!"

"I'll be ready!"

As Suzy's husband slowly opens his sleepy eyes, he sees his wife frantically pulling on her clothes and combing her hair. He marvels at how youthful and energetic she looks.

Where did Suzy get all that energy? It came from her desire to participate in something that brings her enjoyment. Once again, until a married woman enjoys having sex, there is no way to determine her level of desire.

Fortunately, I get the opportunity to speak from both sides of the fence. I remember when having sex once a month was more than sufficient for me. And to make it more interesting—even at that, I wanted Frank to take me to dinner and send me flowers. But when God freed me up to celebrate in His sexual creation, my desires became totally different.

Men are sexually stimulated by what they *see*. But women are essentially stimulated by what they *hear*. And a woman's hearing not only comes from what the man says, but what she hears in her mind concerning sexual intimacy.

If her mind is saying, "Sex is dirty," "Sex is a duty," or "Sex is not godly," she will have a very difficult time responding to her husband enthusiastically. But once she accepts the reality that sex was created by God, that it is good and intended to be enjoyed, it frees her up to begin the process of discovering God's plan for sex.

Getting Ready

There are a few practical things we can do to make sex even more appealing to each other. We live in a world of sights and sounds that affect the way we feel, think, and act. With that in mind, a couple should devote some energy towards sexual preparation. Usually the bedroom is where the sexual act takes place so attention should be directed towards preparing the room.

Tom and Jeannine Gonzales, the marriage counselors that worked with Frank and me in our early years of marriage, once told us that the bedroom was for two purposes: sex and sleeping. Anything that did not relate to those two acts should be removed. They were speaking of the computer and other work-related materials (did I just hear a groan?), beepers, CB radios, and other such paraphernalia.

Now, let's look at personal preparation. Although you probably already know this, I think it also deserves a gentle reminder. Physical cleanliness is of utmost importance to a satisfying sexual experience. One woman complained to me about her husband's bad breath. It was years before she could tell him because she didn't want to hurt his feelings. There are internal and external products that help relieve that problem. Deodorants and soaps help other problems, and fragrances, lotions, and oils bring their own sensual ambience to the occasion.

Developing an Understanding

Frank

Women learn one set of false assumptions about duty and dissatisfaction; men learn another. As a youngster growing up in a large family, it was natural to want to know where all those brothers, sisters, and cousins came from. Did someone win them in the lottery or what? When I quizzed my mother about the origin of babies, she sweetly told me that the stork brought them.

Of course it didn't take long for me to figure out that babies and sex had much in common because I was firmly instructed never to "make babies." In fact, that warning was my complete orientation about sex while growing up at home. But boy was I—along with John and Charles and James and Donnie and Dwight and Henry and Calvin and Johnny and Jack and Richard and Ray and Paul—curious! These buddies and I spent a good deal of our young lives investigating the subject in some detail—but Bunny will be the first to tell you I didn't learn much.

What I did learn was: premarital sex is dirty, dangerous, sin-ful, and fun, and it should be avoided for any number of reasons. Several of my buddies were encouraged by their fathers to get it out of their systems before they got married. The idea was that then they would be true to their wives. Well, I don't have to tell you that most of them have been married at least twice.

God's plan for sex was and is procreation, intimacy, and recreation. It is to be enjoyed by everyone—within the bonds of matrimony. Satan's counterplan for sex is fleshly stimulation, self-adulation, and spiritual annihilation. What I mean is this: When one's principle attraction to sex is for his or her flesh to be stimulated, the natural conse-quences are sexual addictions and reckless perversions. Eventually, neither pornographic displays of erotic es-capades nor fantasy-manipulated masturbation will be enough to satisfy an appetite that is out of control. When self-satisfaction is the principle attraction to sex, lust rules the roost and love is stillborn.

God meant for the act of sex to be both physical and spiri-tual (1 Corinthians 6:19). When we are unaware of the presence of God during the act of sex, our minds are com-pletely open to the assaults upon our spirits by the enemy. Lewd language begins to replace love language; vulgar fan-tasies eclipse precious romantic journeys into the mysteri-ous ways of love.

God is present both as a witness and a participant while we celebrate love and our spiritual heritage.

In Genesis 4:1, Eve says, "...with the help of the LORD I have brought forth a man."

In Genesis 18:10, God says to Abraham, "I will surely re-turn to you about this time next year, and Sarah your wife will have a son."

Genesis 18:12 says, "So Sarah laughed to herself as she thought, 'After I am worn out and my master is old, will I now have this pleasure?'"

Malachi 2:15 says, "Has not [the Lord] made them one? In flesh and spirit they are his. And why one? Because he was seeking godly offspring. So guard yourself in your spirit."

After God had filled an innate need in Adam's life by fashioning Eve for him, Adam's response in Genesis 2:23 was, "This is now bone of my bones and flesh of my flesh."

Finally, Adam thinks, *someone feels like I feel and is the same as I am. Someone can know me and I can know her. Together we are destined to become one flesh. What a blessing!* That is why Paul says, "He who loves his wife loves himself" (Ephesians 5:28). And that not only applies to the beginning of matrimony, but continues through our marriage journey. Proverbs 5:18,19 bears repeating in reference to this lasting quality in marriage:

> Let thy fountain be blessed: and rejoice with the wife of thy youth. Let her be as the loving hind and pleasant roe; let her breasts satisfy thee at all times; and be thou ravished always with her love.

This describes a couple that is growing together, knowing how to reach the highest peaks of emotional and physical oneness together. After surveying several concordances I believe this means that through time (from the time she was a loving hind, until she becomes a gentle roe) a comfortable satisfaction develops which comes only from two people who are committed to being together. And because of this lifelong commitment to becoming one, we can apply Proverbs directly to us:

> Let your wife's breasts satisfy you at all times (concentrate on her breasts being the perpetual source of your contentment—an expression of intimacy and of making love). Allow your mind to become enraptured, intoxicated with the delight of what happens each time you experience one another in the marriage bed.

This love is a love which delights in coming together sexually. This is the same coming together which Paul speaks of in 1 Corinthians 7:5, where he states: "Do not deprive each other." Of course, instructing husbands and wives not to deprive each other is a long way from the tender relationship described in Proverbs 5:18,19. The love spoken of in Proverbs is an intimate love, an ardent and passionate inclination of the mind, a sweetness of affections. This kind of love develops over time.

Bunny and I are still discovering how wonderful it is to have intimacy in a relationship. True intimacy demands honesty ("The man and his wife were both naked, and they felt no shame"). Each one is able to share openly without worrying about hurting the other's feelings, experiencing rejection, or having a sense of inadequacy.

During the act of sex, either Bunny or I may respond "Thank You, Lord!" for at least two reasons. First, we are experiencing the incredible enjoyment that comes when there is no shame or fear. Our bodies and souls are open to one another to explore and enjoy. When sex is enjoyed within the parameters established by God, both the flesh and the spirit are liberated to soar. Second, we recognize that God is indeed present.

In light of His presence, let me also suggest that you and your spouse think about developing a love language for the intimate parts of your body (not like those that have been passed down in back alleys and porn movies). Remember, "old things are passed away; all things are become new" (2 Corinthians 5:17 KJV).

Sex is meant for procreation, intimacy, and recreation. But it also provides relaxation, conversation, and edification. After a long hard day at work, it is refreshing to have a spouse who knows how to create a romantic aura that is scintillating to your libido and tantalizing to your innate need to love and be loved.

Sex is most enjoyable when needs are being met—physically, emotionally, and psychologically. That is to say, when the drive to be sexually satisfied is exceeded by the desire to satisfy, divine spiritual principles are ignited.

Mutual Gratification

Do you remember the last time you went to a crowded restaurant for dinner? You probably waited more than an hour for a table. Once you were seated, the order was taken and still you had to wait another 30 minutes for the main course to be served. Even though you may have been tired of waiting, the meal was so incredibly delicious that you dined enthusiastically. Long after the food was consumed, memories of its taste lingered on. In your satisfaction, you exclaimed, "This meal was well worth the wait!" You then whipped out a larger-than-usual tip for the waiter and another tip for the chef as you happily exited the restaurant. You were satisfied, the waiter was satisfied, and so was the chef. This principle is called mutual gratification.

If the above scenario was about sex instead of dinner, I would have ended it with, "and they happily fell asleep in each other's arms." Too often this is not the case. Many individuals in marriages are so self-serving they are interested primarily in their own self-satisfaction. Of course the problem which this creates is the same problem which Paul warned us about in 1 Corinthians 7:5. "Do not deprive each other" speaks of sexual satisfaction as a goal. The goal of sex, the act itself, is the orgasm. If only one partner is consistently satisfied, then the other partner is being neglected. This exposes him or her to satanic suggestions and temptations.

God's plan for sex in marriage suggests that even if one partner is tired, the anticipation of love's enjoyment through sexual intercourse should arouse them. And long after it is completed, memories of its satisfaction should linger on. As they lie enfolded in each other's arms, both sigh and remember, "It was well worth the time."

The Combination Lock

Bunny

God seems to have created our bodies like a safe with a sexual combination lock. Understandably, everyone has a different combination because God did not make any two things exactly alike—not a snowflake, not the leaves on a tree, not our finger or handprints. One side of every person's face is even different than the other. It stands to reason God would never make two entire bodies the same. Here is a challenge: We alone know our sexual combination, and the only way our husbands or wives are going to learn it is if we reveal it to them.

At this point, you might be thinking, "I don't have a clue as to my sexual combination." Oh yes, you do. Once you accept the fact that sex is good and it is yours to enjoy, you are then free to acknowledge what *feels* good to you. There are certain things your husband does or specific places he touches that bring you special enjoyment. It's up to you to let him know.

Please don't say, "I could never do that! I am too shy or inhibited." If that's your reaction, my suggestion is that you play the hot-and-cold game. If his touch in certain places is not pleasing simply say "cold." There may be places that aren't so bad, so you say "warm." But then there are certain sensations that are, very simply, "Hot, hot, hot!"

Once you begin to explore each other's body in that way, sex becomes an adventure of discovery. God's mercies are new every day and so is the way we feel. Changing moods and times of the month make us feel different. That is why it is not necessary to sit around and fantasize about sex in order to be aroused. All you need to know is that sex is good; it is a celebration of God's creation. And every time you come together, the ultimate result is that you both will be satisfied.

Does complete mutual satisfaction happen in one encounter? No. The fun part is the journey. The sexual act will never become old. It continues to be new as we daily change and develop mentally, emotionally, and physically. Just knowing the experience will be enjoyable causes us to desire it, no matter whether we are happy, sad, energetic, tired, or stressed. We know the end result will be wonderful. Over the years, Frank has been learning my various combinations as I have been learning his. We are both grateful for God's gift of sexual freedom and pleasure.

Lover of Your Soul

It's important to remember that the sexual experience is divinely blessed in marriage. Of course some will say that it was physically satisfying before marriage, but there's a downside to that. First, it broke God's heart; it grieved the Holy Spirit, and it should have caused guilt. Second, depending on what you were involved in doing, it also may have created confusion once you were married. It's probably safe to say that you knew what you did was wrong, so, once married, the confusion begins when you try to enjoy sex—but it reminds you of your wrongdoing. There is a sense of guilt even though you know God has now given His blessing.

A single person can have a sexually satisfying experience but that is as far as it goes because sex is so much more than physical. It also involves the soul which is really who we are—our mind, emotions, and will. When we laugh or cry, we do so from our soul. When we have a sexual relationship that is just physical, it grows old after a while and a new partner is sought.

The Bible says Jesus is the Lover of your soul. Do you think He is going to give your emotional combination to just anyone? No, as far as He's concerned, a marriage commitment is required before He will sanctify and set apart the sexual relationship.

God's sexual plan for us is good, healthy, and safe. It also helps prevent adultery. Frank and I have spent years teaching each other our sexual combinations. There is only one man on earth that can satisfy me and that is my husband. Why? Because he's the only one that has my combination. What reason would I have to look elsewhere for satisfaction? God has made Frank the source of my sexual pleasure and that makes him even more special. Likewise, I am his source. When we do things God's way, we have built-in safeguards for our marriages.

Incest, Molestation and Rape

There is one aspect of sexuality that cannot be overlooked. When a partner has been abused sexually it can have a devastating effect on the relationship. When incest, molestation, and rape are mentioned most people automatically think it's in reference to women. However, statistics are beginning to uncover a tremendous number of men who were also physically violated. These acts can have a powerful impact on a person's ability to enjoy a satisfying sexual experience. He or she will most likely view sexual activity as vile and distasteful. And, in far too many instances, the other spouse has never been told about the offenses. Of course, that complicates the situation.

It's important for victims of those terrible acts to accept an important fact: What is *taken* and what is *given away* are two entirely different acts. When you choose to surrender your body to your spouse, God is pleased and wants you to celebrate in His creation. Anyone who has violated you in the past will be judged by God. Therefore, when you forgive him or her you are free to move on with your life and only forgiveness can set you free. (If necessary, you may want to seek professional help to work through your emotions. It's essential, however, that the counselor be a sound Bible-centered professional.)

No longer do any of us—no matter what our backgrounds—need to be imprisoned by Satan's lies concerning the godly act of sex. Sexual pleasure is meant to be discovered, explored, and cherished by every married couple. It is one of God's most priceless gifts.

Assignment

1. Read *Intended for Pleasure: Sex Techniques and Sexual Fulfillment in Christian Marriages* (Revell) by Ed Wheat and Gaye Wheat.

2. Meditate about your attitude towards sex. Where do you see that changes need to be made?

3. Pray for God's help in unlocking your spouse's combination. If you learn one thing each time you have a sexual encounter, just think how much you will know in a year!

4. Study and understand the sexual anatomy of the male and female body.

5. Develop a love language for the intimate parts of your bodies.

6. Make it a habit to keep your body physically clean in preparation for intimacy.

7. Make agape love the standard for sexual satisfaction. Agape love seeks the highest good of the one who is the object of your affection.

5

Scoring Goals

Bunny

The constant droning of the airplane engines was the first thing I heard as I awakened from my nap. Three hours had passed since my flight left New York. Greeted by pitch-black darkness outside my window, I stared into the stillness; no lights were visible anywhere. Pleasant thoughts of seeing Frank, holding my youngest child Gabrielle, and having long discussions with my older children made the time seem to crawl.

As I stared out, something caused me to suddenly imagine the dark glass of the airplane window was a television monitor. The empty space prompted two questions: What if I didn't know when I'd be landing? What if there were no day, week, month, or year that guaranteed when I would arrive? I could sense a slow panic begin to rise. Gone was the excitement of knowing I would see my loved ones shortly. The very thought of an uncertain future seemed to envelop me in hopelessness. I realized the reason I could endure another two hours of this particular journey was because I knew what and who awaited me.

As far as life journeys are concerned, what kind of flight has your marriage taken? Perhaps it has always been daylight, and you've been able to see miles ahead. Maybe it's been dark, but the sun is just beginning to rise on the horizon. Perhaps the sun is dropping quickly behind clouds of despair. Worst of all, you may be looking out a pitch-black window with no lights in the distance.

Whatever your present circumstances, your goal as a husband or wife is to make a fair marriage good or to make a good marriage great or to find hope and encouragement if your marriage seems doomed to crash.

Charting Your Course

Goal-setting has transformed my marriage to Frank. This became clear to me after one particular conversation took place. For quite some time, I had been secretly struggling with a relational issue concerning a friend. Every time I thought it was getting better, it got worse. One day, overcome with despondency, I entered our bedroom where Frank was reclining on the bed. I sat on the edge and said "Frank, I have a dark area in my heart that I haven't been able to shake. I need to share it with you."

Frank immediately turned off the TV, picked up the telephone and activated the answering service. He then turned and said, "Share your heart."

After listening without interruption, he gave me his brief but very important counsel. The emotional cloud rolled away and I was grateful that we had reached a place in our marriage where I could be "open and transparent."

That was a long way from the path we'd taken when we first got married. In those days, it was not unusual to hear Frank respond to one of my observations with, "That's dumb!"

I would downheartedly reply, "That's not dumb, it's just the way I feel." Frank would go on to explain, "Ninety-five percent of the world agrees with me, five percent agrees with you. That's dumb!" Then, as I scurried away into my lonely emotional closet to lick my wounds, my heart would ache to be understood. I longed for Frank to want to know me.

So what happened? How did he stop saying, "That's dumb!" and start saying, "Share your heart"? Well, I can quickly tell you it didn't happen overnight. But it did happen because of goals.

Frank

The Bible teaches oneness as God's goal for every marriage. That doesn't mean the wife becomes like the husband or the husband becomes like the wife. God's goal is that, within the marriage, both of them become like Christ.

I remember in the first *Rocky* movie, Adrianne's brother asked Rocky, "Hey, Rocky, what do you see in my sister?"

Rocky replied, "I got gaps, your sister's got gaps, together we fill each other's gaps." Isn't that, in large part, what marriage is about—filling one another's gaps? We should be able to reveal our gaps without the fear that our weaknesses will be used against us in a disagreement.

One worthwhile marital goal should be to practice building each other up on a daily basis, edifying one another when one of you is lacking in skill or confidence. Learn to become a sensitive sounding board. While your husband or wife shares a personal concern, you can also pray. This will enable you to receive from God whatever your spouse is trying to say or discover whatever he or she needs to hear.

Step by Step

Bunny

As Frank said, the first goal of marriage is oneness.

The second goal is to make sure, through prayer and Scripture study, that God's instructions and wisdom will accompany you along the journey.

The third goal is to take your hands off the throttle and put your spouse under the control of the all-knowing automatic pilot, Jesus. Haven't you tried hard throughout the years to fix your relationship? You have probably tried flying low, high, through the clouds and storms only to discover that you are in a constant state of turbulence. There is a popular saying that applies to this: "Let go and let God."

I tried all kinds of ways to fix Frank. It was like being on an emotional roller coaster. One day I was kind and pleasant, the next day I was demanding and angry, and on still another day, I was distant and seemingly disinterested.

I vividly remember awaking one morning feeling unappreciated and rejected. How could these feelings be expressed to Frank? How could I start the conversation? While I was staring in the bathroom mirror, a light went on in my creative mind. As my makeup was being carefully applied, I decided to color only one side of my face. Eye shadow and eyeliner were applied to one eye, pink blush was carefully brushed on one cheek and the red lipstick filled in half of my mouth. What a great plan!

Once Frank asked, "Why is your face made-up like that?" I would have the opportunity to blurt out, "I feel unappreciated and rejected and this is my way of getting your attention so you will talk to me more!" Of course, I expected him to feel guilty, and I hoped he would decide that he needed to spend some quality time with me.

Well, as I crawled in the bed and cried myself to sleep that night, I thought about how my wonderful plan had so miserably failed. Not only hadn't Frank noticed, none of my children saw the difference in my makeup either! Another great scheme had bit the dust. I was in even greater despair.

I wonder how many tricks and schemes you have tried to change or improve your relationship with your spouse. My list is long and entertaining. But after I clearly understood God's desire for oneness, I asked Him for wisdom and to order my steps. Letting go of my desire to change Frank was almost as difficult as waiting for God to direct and perform His perfect will in our relationship.

Waiting

Frank often says, "There are no emergencies in heaven." Truly, God's timing is not our own, and when it comes to changing the course of a marriage, He knows that when we are willing to keep our vow "until death do us part," He will have ample time to fix, adjust, and improve us. As I waited on God to change Frank, it amazed me to discover that God's goal was different. His focus was on changing me!

There is a song that says, "Search me, Lord. And if you find anything that shouldn't be, take it out and strengthen me; I want to be right, I want to be whole, I want to be clean...."

When I took my hand off the throttle of the airplane and let God chart the course, He first flew me into self-observance. He caused me to see myself in the light of His Word. I discovered that I was very critical of Frank, sitting in constant judgment. Matthew 7:1,2 came looming into focus on the horizon: "Do not judge, or you too will be judged. For in the same way you judge others, you will be judged, and with the measure you use, it will be measured to you."

That principle was cursing my relationship with my husband, and now I was fully aware of it. I began to understand that "Whatsoever a man [or woman] soweth, that shall he [she] also reap" (Galatians 6:7).

I was planting criticism, judgment, contention, and discord. Yet I was expecting to reap love, romance, and caring. I decided to take my eyes off Frank's perceived shortcomings and concentrate on where I needed to grow. This caused the flight of our marriage to level off. Now it was on a straight, steady course to oneness.

How many times I wanted to grab the throttle from Jesus! But as I practiced keeping my hands folded in my lap and my eyes focused on where I needed to grow, the desire to be in control continued to ebb. And what do you think happened? Frank began to change. Fortunately, he was concentrating on where he needed to grow.

Do It Now

Frank

As you work toward the Master's degree, there are challenges that you will—not may, but *will*—encounter. All along the way you must continue to set realistic and well-defined goals. Goals are important for two reasons. First, they enable you to measure your progress. Second, they minimize discouragement and distractions.

Stop just for a moment and ask yourself these questions:

- What are your goals for your marriage?

- What are your goals for yourself as an individual?

- If you were to draw a picture of what your ideal marriage would look like, how would you describe it?

- What is your spouse's dream for the marriage?

- What are his or her goals in order to reach that dream?

Not having goals for your marriage is like not exercising. When suddenly you are challenged by circumstances to move forward in your relationship, the pain caused by pressure exerted upon unstretched muscles of love may prove to be almost unbearable. Let me elaborate.

Our meeting with James and Patricia was an interesting experience. They had been married for seven years and separated for eight years. Recently, Patricia had felt deeply impressed by the Lord to reunite with James. However, very little had changed upon her return. They still continued to have problems with communication, sex, and finances. Their arguments were known to last for days, resulting in great mental and emotional damage to both of them.

Our recommendation was that James and Patricia set a goal: three months with no arguing. During that time they were to call a truce and commit to each other and to the Lord that they would not quarrel. Whatever problems they currently had would be there in three months, but by then they would have acquired enough information to work through their challenges. Because they lived in another country, we asked them to fax us once a week and give us a report on their progress.

The first week went well. During the second and third weeks, some slight quarrels began to arise. However, when James and Patricia were reminded that their commitment to stop arguing had been made to the Lord as well as to each other, the arguments subsided. When we talked to James, he said, "This is wonderful! For the first time in a long while I woke up and felt like laughing. It's great not wondering when our next argument will occur!"

Setting simple, realistic goals gives us the energy and hope to move forward.

Danny and Susan have been married two years and separated for eight months. Their marriage was in so much trouble that we only set one goal for them: We asked them to commit to pray together on the telephone for 15 minutes every morning—praying for one another's day.

They are keeping that commitment even as this book goes to print and are doing something they haven't done for a long time—talking. That's a baby step, but we believe through their faithfulness that God will add strength to their marital anklebones so they can one day run to victory.

As for our marriage, when it comes to Bunny I know at some point during the month she's going to say or do something that will irritate me. Evil spirits will try and use those little things as a means of building a case against Bunny and her intentions towards me. That's their goal. What is mine?

My goal is to spend time every day admiring something special about Bunny. Perhaps it's the way she smiles or how she blushes when she is embarrassed. Sometimes lying in bed at night, I admire the structure of her cheekbones. Other times, I observe how alluring and captivating she looks as we stroll down the street together in the morning sunlight, her brown eyes concealed behind dark glasses. All the while, I am rehearsing over and over the different reasons why I love her so. In a far broader way, I see as a marital goal the positive principles taught by Paul in Philippians 4:8,9:

> Finally, brothers [and sisters], whatever is true, whatever is noble, whatever is right, whatever is pure, whatever is lovely, whatever is admirable—if anything is excellent or praiseworthy, think about such things....And the God of peace will be with you.

Don't Get Sidetracked

Recently, Bunny and I started out for San Diego, California from our home in Pasadena, driving down Interstate 5 (I-5). It was a clear day and traffic was light until we reached the city of Anahiem. Suddenly it was backed up for miles. I was driving and became irritated and impatient, because it had appeared at the beginning of the trip that this would be an easy journey. Now I was bogged down with no relief in sight. I turned on the radio hoping to catch a forecast of how long this traffic snarl would last. There was no mention of it on the traffic report. Nothing!

Then I saw an exit onto a recently completed freeway feeder. It ran right alongside I-5. Following a few other cars, I swung over to my left and immediately took the exit onto this newly opened roadway. After 20 minutes of steady progress, I suddenly noticed that everyone's taillights were lit ahead of me—and all the cars were starting to U-turn and backtrack.

When I came to the location where every car had turned around, I realized agonizingly that I had been sidetracked. I discovered that we had been traveling on a road which was a dead end. Even though I thought they knew where they were going, everyone ahead of me had recently come to that same conclusion.

Marriage is often the same way. Starting out, couples say to themselves, "Because of our love, this is going to be a piece of cake." But many times when a couple doesn't have a clear view of the road ahead, they are prone to follow the directions of others who are also guessing. (More about that later!) Tragically, they quickly discover that all along they've been on a dead-end road. Usually they don't know that it's a major problem until it's all messed up.

Fortunately, even though I had wasted time on the wrong road, I knew where I wanted to go and that I-5 would take me there. All I had to do was turn around, return to the place where I exited, get back onto the right road and continue until I reached San Diego. Yes, I-5 might still be bogged down, but I knew that sooner or later it would loosen up—it always does.

Each time you are tempted to explode verbally, sulk, entertain adulterous fantasies, or even lie, ask yourself: "Is what I am about to do going to lead me towards or away from our goal of oneness?" The Bible says that patience is a virtue. I now understand with greater clarity what that means.

Other routes may have appeared to be more expedient, but had I remained on I-5 initially, I would not have lost 40 minutes. That lost time caused me to get caught up in the evening rush-hour traffic of five different cities along the way—which I would have missed if I hadn't been delayed. In much the same way, a wrong turn away from the goal of one-flesh can require miles of apologies and years of regret.

One day Bunny said to me, "Frank, I don't feel as though I can be transparent with you." I could have taken off onto that road with a "dead-end" ahead by responding in my usual way, "Why, that's dumb, I don't know why you would say something like that." Instead, this time, I tried listening. What she was saying was, "Frank, I need a relationship with you which allows me to share my heart without fear of being attacked verbally or being belittled. I want a place where I can be honest, where I can convey my hurts and disappointments, as well as my hopes and farfetched dreams. But I'm afraid you can't handle it!" Right then I knew that if oneness was really my goal, and she didn't feel the freedom to share her feelings, then we were heading in the wrong direction.

Have you taken a wrong turn? Stop and think about some of the things that have happened in your relationship that caused you to get sidetracked. What could you have done to affect them? Maybe you were becoming irritated and impatient because you believed, in the beginning, that the journey would be easier? Now you are bogged down with no relief in sight.

If you turn onto a street that proves to be a dead end, as long as you know where you are going and the road that will take you there, you only have to turn around and get back on it. That's why goals are so important. They continually remind us of where we're going.

How to Avoid Falling Apart

So many times I have heard a spouse say, "We just somehow grew apart." Now that is a contradiction in terms if I have ever heard one! How can two people who are both growing, grow apart? Perhaps what the person meant to say is that, "We just fell apart."

I have two lemon trees side-by-side in my backyard. I used to concentrate on watering and feeding one of them because I felt it had the greatest potential for producing fruit. After all, it was already the largest and the healthiest looking of the two. It produces, but not as much as I thought it would. Recently I began to feed and water both of them together. To my amazement, the smaller tree looks as though it is going to out-produce the larger one. Nevertheless, they are both producing and together they are growing.

Likewise, in a marriage where both spouses are being mutually nourished and watered, they grow together. Don't allow your successful career or your education to cause you to see your mate as inferior or inept. As long as you concentrate on nurturing (encouraging and edifying) one another—even though it may be in different pursuits—you will continue growing together and producing fruit.

There have been occasions when Bunny and I have listened to a man or woman unload their marriage problems on us while pointing an accusing finger at his or her mate. As the blame-game continued, and while Bunny and I tried calmly discussing God's plan for their marriage, my insides were screaming, "You are going the wrong way!"

Yet, I realize how hard it can be sometimes. You find yourself sandwiched in between two heavy hitters like Doubt and Discouragement. You are within the grasp of Anger and Resentment. And besides all this, you've just had one too many bad days!

As soon as you can, you are planning to run for daylight. You intend to flee from that broken relationship to run away from all that disappointment and stress. Already you are running hard. But where are you going? You are most likely heading directly into a snare designed by the enemy of your soul, who has set you up. And chances are, he is equally busy tripping your spouse. Often, a person who is in a stressful relationship will run directly into an ungodly relationship.

Maybe all you can see are the challenges facing you, the ones from which you are trying to escape. You're looking at discontentment, at money issues, the sex situation, lack of communication, or at the staleness in your marriage. If that is all you can see, perhaps it is because your eyes are out of focus and you are unwittingly being driven in the wrong direction.

The truth is, those obstacles (which we all encounter) are really road signs along the way to the goal of oneness. Once you have passed them, they become assets. They are there to remind you of the progress you have made toward obtaining your Master's degree.

Stay Focused on the Master

The Holy Spirit alone is able to deliver you to your destination safely. First Thessalonians 5:19,21 says: "Do not put out the Spirit's fire;...Test everything."

Matthew 14:22 tells us about the time that Peter was in a boat with the other disciples in the midst of a turbulent sea. Suddenly they saw Jesus walking towards them on the water. They were terrified because they thought they were seeing a ghost. Jesus immediately allayed their fears by saying to them: "Take courage! It is I! Don't be afraid!"

"'Lord, if it is you,' Peter replied, 'Tell me to come to you on the water.'" What Peter is saying is, "Despite my obstacles, my adversaries, and my adversities, if it is really you tell me I can come to you."

"Come!" Jesus said.

Peter got out of the boat, focused on Jesus and walked on top of the water towards Him. As long as his focus was upon Jesus, he was not afraid. However, when he allowed his focus to shift from the Master to the matter (winds and waves), Peter became afraid and began to sink.

He cried out, "Lord, save me!" Immediately Jesus reached out his hand and caught him. Fortunately, Peter, while sinking, still had enough presence of mind to see that it was he and not Jesus who was sinking, and that Jesus could still rescue him.

What about you? Why not pull off to the side of the road of life right now and say sincerely, "Jesus, if it is You, tell me to come to You." Not only should you "come," but you should also believe that God answers prayer.

Just a Prayer Away

Bunny

My daughter Fawn and I were returning to Los Angeles from Washington, D.C. one hot July day. I encouraged Fawn to take her sweater, because I knew we would be arriving at our destination in the evening. Los Angeles can be hot during the day, but it gets quite chilly at night. Fawn emphatically informed me she would have no need of the sweater.

We arrived at Los Angeles International Airport and, after putting our last piece of baggage on the luggage cart, Fawn and I headed for the exit. As the automatic glass doors opened and the cool air greeted us, I reached for the sweater which I had packed in my purse. Fawn turned her pretty face upward and even before she could verbalize her request, the sweater was on its way to her.

Scripture teaches us that God knows what we need even before we ask. As you turn your face to God and ask for direction in your relationship, you can know that direction is already on its way. Do you think God wants you and your mate to be one? Of course He does. His Word expresses that very desire. In light of that, you can trust—even as you are uttering your request for help—that the answer is on its way.

The difference between my story about Fawn and my experience with God has to do with time. Yes, the answer is on its way but oftentimes it doesn't come immediately. It takes time. There are so many areas in our lives with which we need help. But when we are assured in our hearts that God knows, cares, and answers prayers, it gives us the energy and encouragement to press forward and wait patiently for His intervention.

Journey with a Purpose

Frank

One beautiful December day, Bunny, the children, and I set out from Los Angeles on a journey to Houston, Texas.

Houston is where I grew up, and my mother and many other relatives still reside there. Besides looking forward to the opportunity to visit them, I had also arranged to record an album with a popular Grammy-award-winning gospel group in the area.

Of course, before we started on our journey, we made sure everything was in working order with our automobile. However, after driving five hours we experienced our first mechanical difficulty—the car battery was defective. Once that was repaired, we left Tucson traveling through Arizona into New Mexico.

Halfway through that state we faced another challenge. Apparently, while crossing the desert, we'd hit a dip in the road and bent a tie rod. Our car limped into Las Cruces late in the evening. We checked into a motel and got a good night of rest. Early the next morning we located an auto service center that could repair the problem while we spent a leisurely morning visiting the local sights and shopping. Eventually we were informed that our car was ready to go on the road.

The next eight hours were uneventful, except for an occasional stop for fuel. Then, around 2 A.M. in the middle of a dark, flat plain, we began to experience an electrical shortage problem which caused the headlights to blink steadily on and off. Now that was a frightening experience. One moment we could see everything, the next moment it was pitch black. We were greatly relieved when we hit the city limits of San Antonio. We found a hotel room for the night, and early the next morning we drove the car to the local dealership. They found the problem and fixed it.

By now we were almost at our journey's end. We could feel the excitement and anticipation building as we approached Houston. Finally we saw the skyline of the city, the elaborately constructed freeway system, and the designated sign that would lead us to the community where my mother lived.

Considering all our car trouble, you might well ask the question, "Didn't you feel like giving up and turning around?" My response would be an absolute, unhesitating no. Neither Tucson, Las Cruces, El Paso, nor San Antonio was my final goal. We had to go through those to reach our destination, but *Houston* was our goal. In Houston I would see my brother, mother, sister, and friends I had not seen for years. I would record, hopefully, my next Grammy-award-winning album there. We would also eat some good Texas barbecue.

Yes, we experienced difficulties along the way. But I was more excited about where we were going than discouraged with where we were. Houston was our goal, and behind every goal there is a dream. The bigger the dream the greater the determination to reach that goal. It was true of the Houston trip, and it is true of marriage.

Many things will be done and said which may throw you off track, but making love your aim will always lead you back onto the right road. Paul says in Romans 14:19: "Let us therefore make every effort to do what leads to peace and to mutual edification." That, too, will keep you on the road toward the goal of successful marriage.

Why We Need to Set Goals

Goals keep us heading in the right direction. They minimize distractions and sharpen our focus. Does setting goals indicate a lack of faith in the sovereignty of God? Of course not. Proverbs 21:31 clearly states that "the horse is made ready for the day of battle, but victory rests with the LORD." Therefore, no matter how much we prepare for success, we still must put all of our trust in God's unfailing love.

I encourage you to set short- and long-range goals for your marriage, your family, and yourself each year. Twice a year, sit down and review them. Discuss how you are doing and make adjustments. Sometimes you may have to put your marriage in the shop for repairs, in the hospital for treatment, or in a hotel for rest, but I once heard it said, "If your *why* is big enough, you will figure out *how*." The closer you get to your journey's end, the more you will feel excitement and anticipation build. And the goals you've met along the way will intensify your ultimate joy of receiving the Master's degree.

Assignment

1. Write down what you believe to be your spouse's greatest dream.

2. Write down what you believe to be your spouse's greatest goal.

3. Share that information with him or her to check your accuracy.

4. Make a list of where you would like to be as a couple in one, five, and ten years:
   a. spiritually
   b. financially
   c. physically

5. Select a date (six months away, preferably a weekend) when you can get away to review your goals and to define new ones.

6

$\mathcal{R}$omance, Loving, and Caring

(For Married Men Only)

⌒

Frank

As I watched a recent television talk show, I learned that, as a young man, the actor James Earl Jones had a terrible stutter. Even today he sometimes slips back to his speech impediment. This was astonishing to me! When I think about James Earl Jones, I envision his depiction of the robust and confident heavyweight boxing champion of the world Jack Johnson. And who could appreciate the powerful images portrayed in the Star Wars Trilogy without shuddering at the thunderous voice of the fearsome Darth Vader? Or what about the rich and majestic vocalization of Mufasa in Walt Disney's *The Lion King*? Every one of these magnificent, larger-than-life characters was enlivened by the voice of James Earl Jones.

After thinking about the struggle Jones went through to speak at all—much less to speak with such power and authority—I suddenly caught a glimpse of myself stuttering, fading in and out. In that moment I told myself, "Frank, that's your problem! You may not suffer from a verbal speech impediment, but when it comes to the beautiful language of romance, you stutter!"

The Elusive Butterfly

In novels, one of two ideas of romance is usually revealed. Either a damsel in distress is rescued by her "Prince Charming," charging in on a white stallion or romance is brought to the lovely young lady by some smooth-talking lady-killer, a suave and debonair "Mr. Perfect." As far as I can see, I fit neither one of these descriptions.

Early in my marriage to Bunny, I tried to overcome my deficiency in "rapping," which is what the verbal language of romance was called in my neighborhood. Instead, I endeavored to do spectacular or novel things: finding the special unusual gift, patronizing the most enjoyable places for dinner, unveiling an oddly timed surprise. Anything which lifted my actions towards Bunny above the clichés of romance was the path I chose as my personal language of love.

How did it work? Have you ever watched anyone try to catch butterflies? It can be a frustrating adventure, indeed. The moment you believe the butterfly is in the net, you see it flying away—for some men, romancing a woman can be somewhat the same. It was for me.

Much later, Bunny and I made the decision to truly become "one," and we began to practice the art of open and transparent communication. When we started talking about it, Bunny defined her idea of romance in terms of simple things like going for walks and talking tenderly. Of course I loved holding her easy-to-caress hands and looking into her soft brown eyes. But I always knew that after 20 or 30 steps along the journey of a short walk, I would run out of "sweet little nothings" to say and then she would be bored. So I would go for walks with her only occasionally, usually during a time of traveling or visiting places where we could talk about the scenery or its history.

Bunny also loves to go on picnics. Now picnics aren't something that cause me to leap for joy. Again, I love being with Bunny, but I just don't have a vocabulary of sweet words to dribble off my tongue while we sit on a blanket filled with ants and surrounded by swarming, hungry, and pushy little flies!

Bunny also expressed her desire to visit museums and art galleries. Now I love museums and art, but once I have seen what is there I'm ready to move on. If I'm going to see it again, I'd prefer seeing it in my house on my walls. I do enjoy visiting historic museums when we travel, but if I'm at home in Los Angeles, the only reason I want to seek out new ones and go there is because Bunny is there. This may help to explain why, after 30 years of marriage, we've only been once to the Huntington Library and to the Norton Simon Museum.

One day Bunny told me that another thing she enjoyed along the route of romance's journey to fulfillment was love notes. *Good!* I thought to myself. *That's not the same as trying to put all that I feel for her in words. Writing I can do!* This suggestion was additionally appealing to me because I couldn't recall ever writing love notes to anyone else, so this would indeed be a great way of saying to Bunny, "You are more special to me than anyone has ever been before." For me, romance is finding different ways to say "You are special." And, fortunately, Bunny loves my love notes. She even talks about papering an entire wall in our bedroom with them someday.

Early in our marriage, one of the things I consistently liked to do was to bring home bouquets of flowers of different fragrances and colors. In response, however, Bunny consistently told me she didn't like flowers! "They depress me because after a few days they die," she would say. "And besides, you should spend the money on something I can enjoy long-term."

I stubbornly continued buying flowers until one day a lightbulb came on in my head. I started to bring home live plants! But I also discovered that Bunny doesn't have a green thumb, and they died almost as quickly as the cut flowers. Of course, when I traveled, I always brought her nice things from distant lands. Meanwhile, after many years, flowers and plants have slowly become appealing to her.

After all that, there's one thing I know. During the remaining years of our lives together I will take Bunny, at regular intervals, on picnics, to symphony concerts, on short walks, and to museums. Why? Because I love her. And because, to her, those things represent romance.

Those things mean something to me, too. They represent thoughtfulness. And, in a way, I suppose this is a confession that I haven't been as thoughtful as I could have been. Yes, I look for the novel and spectacular opportunities to say, "You are most special." But if those were my only means of romancing Bunny, I would be wasting a lot of time and money.

What about you? If it is your desire to romance your wife, find out what romance means to her. Don't do the things *you* think are romantic. Do the things that will make your romance sweeter to *her* taste. It could be that she will be delighted simply because you thought of romance—that your effort is pure and simple romance to her. Whatever the case, find out before you spend a lot of unprofitable energy going in the wrong direction.

A Man's Romance

The woman and the man are different in more ways than the most obvious. To love a man, a woman must say in words and actions, "I trust you and I need you." To love a woman, a man must say in words and deed, "I hear you, I long to be near you, and I care." To the woman love and romance go hand in hand. To have one without the other sometimes suggests that you have neither. They are inseparable to her.

On the surface, to a man, romance is a response to subtleties, say, of a lightly perfumed scarf. Or the invitation to a private picnic unfolded upon the floor of a meadow. Somewhere between scenery and substance, romance is born within the heart of a man. But whenever it is allowed to descend to the level of common exchanges, it loses its power.

Most relationships start out with some degree of romance, only to gradually be replaced with activities which shape our personal values and signify practical living. And so the initial romance is soon reduced to gifts at appropriate times, hobbies, and family responsibilities. Yet romance is the avenue which transports the full essence of love to its summit. It carves out its place in the side of that mountain named Desire.

A man is designed to pursue love's prey until bound-up love can finally be unleashed, until it can be given away to grow unhindered, unrestrained. A man longs to explore the farthest reaches of love, to lift up the one who is the object of his pursuit and the aim of his pulse. But a man is often reluctant to completely and unconditionally surrender his heart for fear he may lose himself in the process.

Meanwhile, a woman's greatest need is security: emotionally, physically, economically, and spiritually.

What a predicament! No wonder Proverbs 30:18 says, "There are three things that are too amazing for me, four that I do not understand: the way of an eagle in the sky, the way of a snake on a rock, the way of a ship on the high seas, and the way of a man with a maiden."

This may be an ancient proverb, but this is where the rub is in our current circumstances. The way of a man with a maiden is so mysterious, it must be sought after in order to unlock the secrets of romance.

For the average man it is quite simple. His ego is on the surface, so he can be romantically placated when a woman gives him affectionate attention and consistent affirmations in the areas toward which he directs her attention. In order for a man to successfully romance a woman, he must first understand that her desire is to reveal herself completely to him. However, a woman's vanity characteristically causes her to hide herself, daring a man to dive into the depths of this bottomless domain.

Romance is a necessary component because it shades the landscape of love with brilliant, uncommonly sighted colors which can only be found in the far-reaches of creation—the depths of a woman's heart.

"Where then," you might ask, "should a man begin?" I cannot say completely with confidence that I know the answer. Greater men of pen and ink than I have succeeded in saying in print what they have failed to manifest in person.

What Is Missing?

I suggest we start where I once heard Dr. Clarence Walker, a brilliant young psychologist and teacher, end his presentation one afternoon. Here is what he said: "God made the woman, Eve, out of what he took away from the man, Adam." What did he remove from Adam? A rib. What is the significance of that? The woman is made from "what is missing out of the man."

Because she comes from man, there is a natural attraction between a man and a woman. He pursues and woos her and says in word and deed, "I want you. I am incomplete without you in my life." For a man to romance a woman he must get across to her that she is someone he has been looking for all of his life, and now he has found her. Take, for instance, the following account:

One Sunday evening, Bunny was flying back into Los Angeles from Dallas, Texas. Now I have always loved to prepare some special greeting for her arrival but I don't always get around to doing it. This time, however, she had been gone for a week.

Fawn got the downstairs cleaned up. I had spent a long day at church, arrived home, and made sure the kids had eaten. I then rushed out to the market because I wanted to set the bedroom up with a large, fresh fruit basket and several vases of red, white, and yellow roses. Next I plugged into the electrical outlet a beautiful fragrance of soft potpourri.

Finally, I wrote her a note which expressed only a fraction of what was in my heart. "If I were to fill your room with roses enough to express how much I care for you, we would have to live outdoors."

My efforts were well received, and Bunny was, as always, delighted with my love note. But it wouldn't have been enough for me to simply say it. I always have to get around to proving it.

Now to be sure, some women would settle for a simple marriage proposal. After a while, however, they will have to be reassured that the man is aware that he must continue to pursue her, listen to her, and discover her. Although he may have married her, he still doesn't know how much he is missing.

For example, when a woman says to her husband, "You really don't know me," she is not saying to him, "You're dumb." She is saying, "You don't know me because I haven't told you." Getting to know her requires that she opens up and reveals some things about herself that presently are faint etchings impressed upon her soul. But for her to reveal this, a man has to be patient and listen.

A woman loves to talk about everything, including herself. But often personal talk is sandwiched between different subjects. A man prefers to talk about specific things. But when a man approaches the door of romance with his wife, he is about to enter a chamber which holds in store revelations which show "what is missing from the man."

And what is missing from the man? I have given much thought to this question. Here is my conclusion: I believe that *someone for him to love and someone to love him is what is missing.* As a man's affectionate affirmations and constant attention are directed towards his wife, she senses his commitment; he is building her confidence more and more. She then feels safe and secure enough to become vulnerable and completely transparent, revealing who she is and the way she is. This, then, draws out of him the reason to give to her a love he has never known, already existing inside of himself.

Her trust in him which has grown, now intones reassuringly, "I believe in you, I feel secure in you, protected—satisfied and complete in you. God did His greatest work when He created you, my husband."

Loving

When a man marries a woman, he must understand that she is made to be loved. A woman's greatest need is security. And once she knows she is loved unconditionally, sacrificially, and wholeheartedly, she feels completely secure. Therefore, loving her is the key. And love isn't simply romantic, as important as that is. A woman needs to be able to relax, knowing that she is married to a man who will provide for his family's needs materially, emotionally, and spiritually.

God sent an angel to the house of Joseph, Mary's husband, for the purpose of warning him that the little child, Jesus, was in danger. And it was to Joseph, the husband, that the angel appeared. It must have been quite comforting for Mary, the mother of Jesus, knowing that her husband and God had communicated about the situation their family faced.

God could give instructions which Joseph would follow. It must have equally comforting for Mary to realize that even though her family would have to flee to a foreign country (Egypt)—away from familiar surroundings and available employment opportunities—Joseph would do whatever it took to provide for his family. It was clear that he loved her. When a man loves a woman, he will do for her naturally all the things that he is willing to do for himself. Because as Paul says in Ephesians 5:28, *"He who loves his wife loves himself."*

Let me explain what I think that means. Marriage restores what was separated by God in creation. God took the man, who by himself was incomplete, removed a rib from his side and created a woman. Then He brought the woman back to the man and presented her to him so that he might have someone to love and someone to love him in return; "God saw all that He had made, and it was very good" (Genesis 1:31).

So it is that Paul says, "no one ever hated his own body, but he feeds and cares for it, just as Christ does the church—for we are members of his body" (Ephesians 5:29).

What Manner of Love?

How can a man love his wife emotionally? Sometimes a woman just needs to know her husband hears her. This is not because she wants him to agree with her—or even to understand her perfectly. She longs to know that he genuinely wants her to share what is in her heart. However, the more he takes the time to clear his mind and listen, the more he will understand her.

At other times, an act of love for your wife can be expressed in depth by something as simple as clearing the table after dinner, doing the dishes, or running warm bath water in the tub for her. Often Bunny will express to me how much something like that has blessed her.

A man can love his wife by protecting her from the stress of always having to discipline the children. Be willing to step in and discipline them after she has given them continuous verbal warnings. As you remove her stress through kind, affectionate, understanding love, she will take stress off you through respectful, loyal, supportive love.

First John 4:19 says, "We love because he first loved us." Christ wooed us, then proved to us His love by the sacrifice of His life. You are not asked to give up your physical life for your wife. You are asked to sacrifice your selfishness, your stubbornness, and your fear of being hurt in order to give to her what she needs most—a man who truly loves her.

A woman may prefer that a man surprise her with an action or expression which exhibits a personal sacrifice of time, resources, or creativity. She will quickly recognize it when your actions demonstrate "I love you."

When a man loves a woman, he seeks for the highest good which can be directed towards her, preferably one to which she can say "amen." And, usually, if she says "amen," it is because the man has hit the nail on the head.

When a man loves a woman, he should provide for his own spiritual development and nurture his wife's as well. The benefit of prayer power combined with sound biblical under-standing causes a man who loves his wife to pray with her re-garding issues which could affect both their lives.

Finally, as Paul writes in 1 Corinthians 13:7,8 NKJV:

> [Love] bears all things [protects her reputation, guards her against emotional stress, and so on], believes all things [always looks for the best out of every situa-tion], hopes all things [never gives up hoping], en-dures all things [keeps pressing forward in faith for the victory]. Love never fails.

Caring

Fred gets up each morning and prays for God's grace and guidance for himself and for his family. He washes and grooms himself. He exercises, eats a nutritionally balanced meal, pays attention to his health and, if he is not feeling well, he takes care of it. He dresses in neat, fine-quality attire and drives to work in a well-maintained automobile. He does whatever he can to protect his body and promote his economical, sociolog-ical, and spiritual progress.

Does Fred treat his wife the way he treats himself? The apostle Paul says the husband should care for his wife as Christ cares for the church. He should protect her, nourish her, see that she looks good, and dresses well. Let her drive the nicer, more durable car so that she is least likely to have a mechanical break-down or suffer harm in an automobile accident. Sacrifice if you have to, but try and provide for your wife a maid or housekeep-ing assistance. In Proverbs 31, the section generally known as "The Virtuous Woman" (to which every man would love to be married), describes a priceless wife who had several servant girls.

The late Dr. E.V. Hill often encouraged the men in his congregation to provide household help for their spouses. He said, "When I wanted to marry Baby, I wasn't huntin' for a maid, I was huntin' for a mate...someone I can come home to and she's not more worn out at the end of the day than I am. If I were looking for a maid it would be cheaper to hire one!"

When he made that statement, the congregation burst into laughter with 99 percent of the women shouting choruses of "Amen!"

I hope I have encouraged you, as a husband, to seek new and innovative ways to demonstrate that you care. Consider, for example, Donald's creative efforts.

Christine and Donald have been married for eight years. Growing up in a midwestern rural town, Christine never had the opportunity to dress up in a formal and attend a special event. The only exposure she had to such opportunities was through her grandmother, who had once traveled to France and would often read to her French literature. Meanwhile, when Christine was just five years of age, her father ran off with another woman. His loss left Christine with feelings of vulnerability and low self worth. She stayed mostly to herself.

Donald is a quiet, hard-working man who loves Christine greatly. Soon after meeting her at the county fair, they began to date. She thought he was nice but never harbored any grand expectations for a life of happiness or excitement. To begin with, neither her mother nor grandmother ever had anything good to say about men.

After three years of dating, Donald proposed to Christine and she accepted. The first three-and-a-half years of their marriage produced two daughters, and things seemed fine. Then, poisoned by her mother's tongue and her own experience, Christine's bitterness toward men surfaced. Although Donald did all he could to please her, the cutting remarks and constant belittling of him were becoming almost impossible to bear.

Nevertheless, because Donald cared so much for her, he labored to find his way through the dross of resentment in order to uncover the gold he could see deep within her.

During occasions of lighthearted conversation about nothing really special, his heart ached for her whenever she lamented her plain and simple childhood. This was complicated by the hurt and anxiety she had lived with most of her life. Donald began to notice that each time Christine mentioned the stories her grandmother used to read to her and her longings to experience just once an opera of a French classic, her eyes would light up. Only the reality of her predictable life brought her back down to earth.

Donald began a special vacation fund and subscribed to a Boston and New York monthly magazine which featured entertainment news articles. Shortly thereafter, he found in "Coming Attractions," a very popular opera of a French classic which was scheduled to open in Boston in the fall. This gave him approximately ten months to save.

Although their salaries were meager, from the modest amount left over each month Donald began to set some money aside. He planned for a pair of train tickets to Boston, a hotel room for two nights, dinner, and two tickets to the theater. He encouraged Christine to request her vacation time around the opera season in case he was able to save enough, but he did not tell her why. Reluctantly she agreed to ask her mother to babysit. She also submitted to Donald's desire to travel to Boston, partly because she had only once traveled anywhere outside of her small town.

When they arrived in Boston, Christine was immensely excited. Magazine pictures she treasured in her mind were coming to life before her eyes. The first evening, Donald walked her to a local cafe for dinner, and from there, by taxicab, they traveled to the opera house. When Christine arrived she couldn't believe what she was seeing! And, like the flood of a rising tide dammed up for eternity, she unleashed a river of emotions, crying softly throughout the entire performance. "I never could have imagined this happening to me," she later explained.

In that one evening, Donald proved to her what the Lord had been saying to her most of her life: "Christine, you are special, you deserve to be happy, let me dry the tears of your hurts away."

Peter tells us, "Cast all your anxiety on him because he cares for you" (1 Peter 5:7). Sometimes life can seem to be such a burden and marriage is just an added load. But when a husband is able to demonstrate to his wife Christ's commitment to her, it can make a world of difference in your marriage. So little is necessary to bring so much happiness to someone you love.

Living in Emotional Safety

What an atmosphere of blessedness and total contentment it is to exist in an environment where you are free to reveal who you are and what you feel without fear of condemnation or rejection! To live in such an environment is to be connected to someone who cares for you and accepts you completely and unconditionally. The Bible says, "Love covers a multitude of sins" (1 Peter 4:8). That is how Christ loves us, and it is also how He says husbands are to love their wives.

Of course, it is not easy to love someone who doesn't appreciate you, submit to you, or respect you. But I believe God has created deep within the belly of a man, a strength which responds, "I have enough love for the both of us." It is the same love which flows out of the fountain of grace from beneath the throne of God and empties into us. It is the same love which God demonstrated towards us "in that while we were yet sinners, Christ died for us" (Romans 5:8 KJV). I do not believe that He would have commanded us to love our wives as Christ loved the church unless He has given us men the provision to do so. But we must reach deep down within ourselves and come up with the bouquet of flowers she alone will enjoy.

One evening after work, Lloyd Blue walked into his house and presented to his lovely wife, Tressie, 11 roses. He then excitedly said to her, "Darling, here are 11 beautiful roses I picked just for you. Now, go and stand in front of a mirror and you will have a dozen."

Solomon reminds us in the Song of Solomon 8:7: "If one were to give all the wealth of his house for love, it would be utterly scorned."

Money can't buy love.

Love has to be given away in order for its power to be manifested. A man who learns to love his wife God's way will never worry about not being appreciated, submitted to, or respected. For, in the final analysis, a woman lives to be loved. A man's love is the fire which burns away all anxiety from her heart, all doubts from her mind, and all fears of failure. His constantly demonstrated care for her fans the flames of their love into an eternal blaze.

When Bunny and I first married, I didn't love her. I didn't know how to love her. I was incredibly interested in her, I was enchanted by her, and I greatly desired to spend the rest of my life with her. But love, as I have now learned to live it, and caring, as I have now learned to give it, has taught me to trust God's enduring principles of enrichment for life's fullest meanings.

A Prologue for Romance

Allow me to provide for you a glimpse into the heart of my wife for her view of a romantic rendezvous. Imagine if you will, early one morning I arise and hurriedly travel two blocks from my house into a slightly rustic area. On a neighborhood walkway I see a rock underneath which I plant a love note. I then return home and invite Bunny to go for a walk. As I near the area where the rock conceals my note to her I ask, "What's that sticking out from underneath that rock?" I go to the rock, pull out the note and read it to her. That, my friend, guarantees good loving for the next two weeks at least!

Romance, the kind upon which I am presently focusing, is elusive for it is the spark which lights the passionate flame of love. Even when nights are cold and damp and summer has fled the room, one true blast from the horn of romance and spring is in full bloom.

Romance is a picture promise which resolves to meet all of the loved one's needs. Romance seeks to plumb the mysterious ways of love and bring to the surface its truest meanings. Romance stretches the boundaries of reason and never bothers to stop and answer the question, "Why?"

Why don't you try having dinner by candlelight; then a warm bubble bath, accompanied by a soft blue light; a quiet serenade under the stars and moonlight as you sift through countless expressions and trivial pursuits looking for just the right word and the right way to say: *I love you.*

Points to Remember

- Romance seeks to say in words and deeds, "You are special!"
- A woman loves and needs to be romanced.
- Romance is the language of love.
- To a woman, love and romance go hand in hand.
- Woman is made out of what is missing from man.
- What is missing from the man is someone for him to love and someone to love him.
- A husband's love seeks the highest good that can be directed towards his wife.
- A husband must seek ways to demonstrate to his wife his awareness that she is a precious vessel.
- Caring continues to show concern for whatever matters to the one cared for.
- Romance stretches the boundaries of reason and never bothers to stop and answer the question, "Why?"
- God would not have commanded husbands to love their wives like Christ loved the church without giving men the provision to do so.
- Let God's Spirit show you how to romance your wife.

Assignments

1. Choose a special moment and ask your wife, "What are things I can do for you that you would consider romantic?"

2. Write down her answers.

3. Commit to practicing one romantic venture each month.

Midterms

1. What are three characteristics of oneness?

   _____
   _____

2. What does one into one equal?

   _____
   _____

3. How does being one help in prayer?

   _____
   _____

4. Where are you on the graph of oneness—going away from or toward your spouse?

   _____
   _____

5. What are strongholds in disguise?

   _____
   _____

6. When do you know you are in a spiritual battle?

   _____
   _____

7. Where is the devil's favorite playground?

    _____

    _____

8. Write an episode of conflict experienced between you and your mate. List the problem and the steps you must take in order to overcome it and be victorious.

    _____

    _____

9. What are some of your excess baggage? How can you eliminate them from your life?

    _____

    _____

10. What are ways in which we communicate?

    _____

    _____

11. Ask a close and honest friend to rate your style of communication. On a scale of 1–10 (10 being highest and positive, 1 being lowest and negative), what number between one and ten best represents you consistently?

    _____

    _____

12. Plan to work on and raise your communication rate quarterly (see question 11).

    _____

    _____

13. Patience is a _____, according to Scripture.

14. Often a person who is in a stressful relationship will run from that one and fall directly in an_____
_____ relationship.

15. I need to stay focused on the_____.

16. Why do we need to set goals?

    _____

    _____

17. The woman is made for_____.

18. The man is made for_____.

19. To refuse to forgive a person from a debt they cannot pay is to hold yourself in emotional bondage and under physical duress.   True   False

20. God has tied together obedience to Him and blessings from Him.   True   False

21. What represents romance to your spouse? Make a list.

    _____

    _____

22. Why is romance so important in a marriage?

    _____

    _____

23. What does romance seek to say in so many ways?

    _____

    _____

$\mathcal{R}$espect, Loyalty, and Support

(For Married Women Only)

Bunny

Frank painted an exquisitely beautiful portrait of romance, loving, and caring in the last chapter. And those elements cause a woman to blossom into a beautiful flower. In a parallel way, the respect, loyalty, and support a wife provides for her husband gives him the strength to be the stem that holds up the blossom. Understanding these three basic and important principles can prevent that stem from being bruised or broken.

School's in Session

Did this happen to you? At ten years old, you awakened to the sound of laughter and warm conversation between your mother and father. As you sat down at the breakfast table and your father said grace, he thanked God for your mother and asked God to bless her talents and her day. Over breakfast your mother said to you, "Honey, I hope you know just how special your father is. How fortunate we are to have him as the leader in our home!" Throughout the meal, each of your parents looked for ways to share words of encouragement and love with each other and with you.

I hope that was the way your family functioned. Unfortunately, my guess is it was not! And if the art of respecting the husband was not exemplified in your childhood, where would you learn it? Finding a positive model for that particular skill could be like searching for a needle in a haystack. Wifely respect for husbands is rarely practiced in our society. In fact, in some circles it is looked upon with disdain.

We have to be willing to unlearn incorrect teachings, leave behind bad role modeling, and educate ourselves on how to properly apply God's Word to our marriages. That is why we have to work with the same intensity as a person going for an earthly master's degree. Not only are the principles of respecting, being loyal to, and supporting a husband foreign to most women, they fly in the face of the feminist movement which wields considerable power over our thinking.

I have a great deal of admiration for my husband's desire to learn how to love me properly. If you and your husband are working through this book together, you need to stop and thank God for your husband's willingness to discover how to love you from God's point of view (even if he continues to fall short in some areas). This is not an easy process. So many bad habits and misconceptions have to die.

If you are dealing with this material alone, allow God to repair those areas in your heart, mind, and actions that do not line up with His desire for a healthy marriage. Take your eyes off your spouse and let God deal with him in His time and in His way. Right now, let's focus our attention on how God created husbands to function—according to His design.

Respect

The newly purchased VCR was hooked up and ready to be tested, making the family room complete. I smiled at the sight of my four-year-old daughter settling down to watch her *Snow White* video. Of course, we all assumed that the videoplayer would play videos—that was its intended function.

Wouldn't it have been ridiculous if I had started complaining about the videoplayer not being able to play cds and cassettes? How strange if I had insisted on writing to the manufacturer, complaining because their VCR equipment did not have other capabilities. Of course, that was not how the manufacturer designed the product; our new VCR was operating properly based on how it was built.

As silly as that may seem, wives have a tendency to do the same thing with God's design of our husbands. Many women have difficulty with God's specifications and manufacturing skill. God constructed our mates with, among others, three very basic needs: respect, loyalty, and support. These are as necessary to him as romance, loving, and caring are to wives. Unfortunately, not enough of us take the time to understand the operating instructions (the Bible) concerning the proper handling and care of one of God's most precious gifts—husbands. With proper understanding and application, there will be no need to trade in what we have for a newer model.

Just what is respect? The dictionary says: "To hold in high esteem; regard." When you respect someone it dictates your attitude and actions towards him or her. Have you ever noticed how the tone of your voice changes when you are in the presence of someone you hold in high regard? Whether it's in church, on your job, at school, or with a family member it is an automatic response—no classes or instructions are necessary. Even a rebellious teenager who shakes her fist at the world becomes meek and humble in the presence of a recording star she admires. Our whole countenance is affected when respect is in operation.

What about your response to your spouse? Ask the Holy Spirit to replay conversations you have had with him within the last three days. Focus on each one. Was it respectful or hostile? Was it kind or contentious? Was it patient or demanding?

Does respect dictate the tone in which you address your husband? Some of you may respond, "Well, Bunny, you don't know my husband. I would respond with respect if he acted differently!"

Jesus addressed that statement in His discourse commonly known as the beatitudes. He said in Matthew 5:46: "If you love those who love you, what reward will you get? Are not even the tax collectors doing that?"

As followers of Jesus Christ, the difference between our responses and those of unbelievers is that we do the right thing regardless of the actions of another person. No, it is not easy. But God's Word tells us:

Bless them that curse you (Matthew 5:44 KJV).

A soft answer turns away wrath (Proverbs 15:1 NKJV).

When you give good things to your enemy, it is like pouring hot coals of fire on his head (Proverbs 25:22).

Am I suggesting that your husband is your enemy? No. But if those Scriptures hold true for someone who does hate you, how much more effective are they with someone who cares about you? God has equipped you with some effective weapons against insults, rude behavior, and verbal abuse. The challenge is that we are supposed to die to our old ways of responding, choosing instead to obey God's Word.

Reverence

God not only calls the married woman to respect her spouse, He takes it to an even higher level with the principle of reverence. Ephesians 5:33 (KJV) reads: "[Let] the wife see that she *reverence* her husband" (emphasis added).

Since my brother and sister-in-law, Cliff and Audree, were married in 1968, they have faced tremendous struggles. When

Audree surrendered her life to Jesus in 1975, she wanted to learn how to love Cliff according to God's Word. That was not an easy task. He was often critical, self-centered, and controlling. When he spoke to Audree, his tone was frequently condescending and curt.

Nevertheless, Audree began to reverence Cliff in her attitude and actions. There were many days when she walked away with tears streaming down her face as she committed herself to loving him God's way. Gradually, as the years passed she began to notice changes in Cliff's behavior. Meanwhile, my brother was amazed that he was no longer able to rattle his wife whenever he had the whim to do so. Audree had discovered peace in the midst of many unpleasant circumstances. She had found contentment in spite of her husband's actions. She continued to study material that would strengthen her resolve and heal her from past hurts.

Seven years later, Cliff became seriously convicted concerning his actions and attitudes not only toward Audree but toward others as well. He knew counseling was needed but who could he trust? One day he approached Audree and said, "Honey, I know that I need help. You're the most godly person I know. Would you be willing to counsel me?"

Audree is a trained counselor, and she replied, "Yes, Cliff, I am willing. However, if you do not do your homework assignments and whatever is required in order for you to be whole, I will immediately stop and turn you over to another counselor. Because above all things, you are my husband and I will honor you in that role."

Today Cliff is the pastor of an exciting, fast-growing church. He and Audree work side by side and many have come to know Christ in a deep and sincere way through their testimony. Audree understood the principle of reverence, which amounts to ultimate respect. There is only one other person in the Bible that we are called to reverence and that is God. So, in a sense, God chose to share His glory with the married man.

Perhaps this idea is causing feelings of resentment to rise within you. Didn't God know the shortcomings and flaws of husbands when He decided to bestow that honor? The answer is most definitely yes, and in His wisdom that was still His choice. Never has Proverbs 3:5,6 been more appropriate:

> Trust in the LORD with all your heart *and lean not on your own understanding;* in all your ways acknowledge him, and he will make your paths straight (emphasis added).

We can go on forever speculating why God requires wives to reverence their husbands. Or we can decide to live up to God's desire and surrender our will and obey His Word. The truth is, ladies, we fall so short in this area that there is no way we can sit in judgment of our husband's deficiencies. This principle is like touching first base on the way to homeplate. If we aren't willing to tag first base, we will never be on the scoreboard.

Calling 911

For almost an hour, I had been fielding calls from single men and women regarding my book *Knight in Shining Armor.* The last caller on the live radio talk show was a young man. The pleasant sounding gentleman said, "I know you've been talking to singles, but I have a marriage question. What if there is someone of the opposite sex who wants to be friends with a spouse? They have long telephone conversations concerning spiritual issues. Do you think it is appropriate?"

I wasn't sure whether a female was calling him or a male was calling his wife. So my response was, "The marriage vow says, 'forsaking all others and cleaving only to the wife [husband].' For every conversation that is taking place with someone of the opposite sex, that is one less conversation that spouse could be having with his or her husband or wife."

The caller emphatically stated, "I told her that!"

Chuckling, I responded, "Well, I wasn't sure who you were referring to and it's unfortunate that this program is not being taped so she can hear the answer."

He laughed and answered, "Oh, she's in the next room listening!"

Since she was listening, I encouraged the wife to ask herself a question, "Why would a man be calling a married woman for spiritual advice? Surely there are plenty of men who could talk to him, including his pastor. That really makes his intentions suspect."

What I didn't say—and it is the crux of the situation—is that this wife was showing disrespect for her husband and probably didn't know it. God designated the husband as the spiritual head of the home. For a man to bypass the husband to speak to the wife was disrespectful both on his part and her part, unless she had received the blessing from her husband to have the conversation. Of course, some husbands do not take the role of spiritual leader in the home. That is one of many areas in which the wife must pray for her husband and let go—giving the process up to God.

More Than a Notion

In my book *Liberated Through Submission*, I describe the agony I experienced when I tried to work through the godly principle of reverence. One particular day, God convicted me about my actions and attitude towards Frank. I knew I was wrong. Sitting in our bedroom rocking chair, I opened the Bible and my eyes went directly to the Scripture, "[Let] the wife see that she reverence her husband." After looking up the word reverence in the dictionary and seeing that it meant "a deep awe," I went to God for an explanation.

Like so many other encounters with the Lord, He spoke softly into my heart and challenged me to think of a person for whom I had a great deal of respect. I immediately thought of my pastor. God then flashed pictures into my mind of my attitude and actions toward him. No one had to teach me what type of tone to use when I addressed him—that was dictated by my respect. Even in times when I didn't agree with something he said or did, I would give it serious consideration before bringing it up. Then, if I did bring it up, my attitude was respectful.

Once I understood the picture of respect, God instructed me to take that respect, multiply it by 100, and give it to my husband. Fortunately, I had great respect for Frank. But what about women whose husbands are unrespectable? I questioned the Lord, "What does a wife do then?" The answer came, "Even if she does not respect the man, she must reverence his position."

I asked the Lord to give me an example so I could understand that principle. He brought to my mind the president, who at that time was Ronald Reagan. When President Reagan walked into congress there were Republicans present who loved his politics and agenda. There were Democrats who were directly opposed to almost anything he wished to do. Some even detested him. But when President Reagan walked into Congress what did everyone do? The answer is simple. They all stood up.

Did they stand for Reagan the actor? Did they stand because Ronald Reagan had no faults? Of course the answer is no. They stood because he was the President of the United States; they stood because of his position. In the same sense, God calls on us to reverence our husbands, not because we think they qualify, but because God bestowed that position upon them.

What does that kind of reverence look like? Do we have to stand up when they walk into a room? No. But I believe our spirits should bow in adoration and respect toward God's selected leader. When that happens our attitude and actions are immediately affected. The tone in which we speak, the way in which we listen, the attitude in which we respond are all impacted by the reverence we hold in our heart.

A Commitment to Reverence

As I sat and meditated on past conversations I'd had with Frank, tears began to roll down my face. I remembered not looking at him when he spoke, cutting him off in the middle of sentences, and using manipulative tactics to get my way. These were just a few of the disrespectful acts I had committed against my husband. I bowed my head and said, "God, from this day forward I will not be irreverent towards Frank—not in words, thoughts, or actions. And if I fall short, I will be quick to apologize to him."

That commitment was followed by a soundless hush that swept over my soul and stayed with me for days. The quiet inside me was beyond my comprehension; it was a silence I could not describe. After a period of time, I realized that I had stilled all the contentious conversations that I'd been carrying on in my imagination. I realized that a great part of my day had been spent arguing with Frank in my mind. No wonder I would be mad when he walked into the room at the end of the day. Sometimes even when we had not had a conversation! I had involved him in angry conflicts throughout the day, and he was not even present.

Respect (reverence) is not an elective course in our quest for our Master's degree. We learn the importance of respect when we read 1 Peter 3:3-7 KJV:

> [Wives] whose adorning let it not be that outward adorning of plaiting hair, and of wearing gold, or of putting on apparel; but let it be the hidden man of the heart, in that which is not corruptible, even the ornament of a meek and quiet spirit, which is in the sight of God of great price. For after his manner in the old time the holy women also, who trusted in God, adorned themselves, being in subjection unto their own husbands: even as Sara obeyed Abraham, calling him lord: whose daughters ye are, as long as ye do well, and are not afraid.

The meek and quiet spirit referred to in this passage of Scripture does not mean you can't talk or have an outgoing personality. It means that your inner spirit is at peace; it means that everything around you can be falling apart but your spirit remains quiet and calm. The Scripture also says that type of spirit is very valuable to God. What makes something very valuable? It's rarity. And the opposite of a meek and quiet spirit is a loud and raging one.

In fact, I once had a loud and raging spirit myself. Externally, I seemed to have it all together, but inside I was fuming. Today, after talking to countless wives, I know I wasn't alone.

Some women have asked me, "How do you get a reverent spirit?" My answer is, "You make a decision." Even though I have to remind myself on a continuous basis, and there are times I fall short, I have decided to reverence my husband. And when I am obedient there is an incredible peace in my marriage. A woman has a tremendous amount of influence in dictating the overall spirit of the marriage and the home. When we accept that truth, it gives us a glimpse of the power that God has placed in our hands. It allows us to rest in the knowledge that He is moving—even when there is no apparent change.

Loyalty

As you go for your Master's degree in marriage, what grade would you get in the course called "Loyalty to Your Husband"? Do you ever discuss your husband and your marriage problems with friends and family? That is disloyal. First of all, a husband usually knows that these conversations are taking place, and he feels ashamed and betrayed. We should do everything in our power to protect our husband's heart and reputation.

Some wives ask, "Well, just who can I talk to? I've got to talk to *somebody!*" They feel that if they don't have the opportunity to vent their frustrations, they will suffer emotional and mental harm. If you have the need to share your marital problems with someone, make sure it is with a qualified biblical counselor. Our family and friends are generally ill-equipped to give us sound advice. To make matters worse, long after we have forgotten the conversation, they may continue to hold a grudge against our spouse.

I remember when I worked outside the home how loyal I was to my employers. I prided myself in anticipating the needs of my boss. Yet, in those earliest years of our marriage, when Frank asked me to do the smallest task, I did it with great reservation and halfheartedness. How unfortunate that I would give 100 percent to someone who had not committed to love, honor, and cherish me until death do us part. Can you see how destructive and ungodly that pattern of thinking and action is?

Of course, on our jobs we get a pat on the back and hear, "Well done!" We also get a paycheck. And yes, there are many things that we do for our spouses that seemingly go unnoticed. But let me encourage you to remember that God is recording every good work. The Scripture urges us not to be discouraged in doing well, for we will receive a just reward.

When a husband receives respect, loyalty, and support he is built-up in the inner man. The conquering male spirit endowed to him by the Lord is stimulated to do bigger things—to climb higher mountains, to accomplish greater successes. Your God-given gift of female influence is at its best when you exercise these principles with your spouse.

Support

When I speak of a wife's support of her husband, I am not talking about financial or physical support. What I mean by support is encouragement. Our husbands long to know that we appreciate and need them. Sometimes when we see the word "need" we think it means that we can't make it without them. For the most part both the husband and wife know that is not true. When a woman says to the husband, "I need you," she displays a humility that communicates, "You are my life. There are areas in my heart that can be filled only by you. You are the covering that God has placed over my life, and I need you to help me become all God has created me to be. I need you emotionally and physically. You are the love of my life."

When I've asked husbands, "Do you feel respected and needed by your wife?" many have answered me with a firm no. Their pain is evident, although at times it is masked by a seemingly distant and uninterested attitude. They are extremely fearful about letting their wives see their vulnerability. They don't feel safe.

Just as we wives need their love and care, our husbands need our support. They should feel sure that we are in their corner 100 percent. Even when they make mistakes (which they are guaranteed to do because they're not perfect), we should have the faith to believe God can repair the damage.

Our former pastor, E.V. Hill, and his wife, Jane, have both passed away. But during their marriage she set a wonderful example of support and encouragement for her husband. Shortly after they were married, her husband invested all their money in a gas station. Jane did not agree with his decision because she felt he did not have the expertise or time to run that type of business. One day he called home to let her know the business had failed. When he explained that he had lost all their money, she simply replied, "Oh, all right."

When he came home, she could have browbeat him, saying "I told you so!" Instead, she sat him down and said, "Listen, you don't drink or smoke. I've done some calculating. If you had both of those expensive habits, you would have spent as much money on that over the years as you did on the gas station. It seems to me that you're even."

A short time later, Pastor Hill came home one evening to a house full of lit candles. He asked Jane, "What meanest thou by this?"

She replied, "Well, I thought it would be nice if we had dinner by candlelight."

When he went to the bathroom to wash his hands, he flicked the light switch and nothing happened. He then went from room to room doing the same thing, and quickly realized that the electricity had been turned off. Jane began to cry and explained that she didn't want him to be discouraged because he worked so hard.

Once again, she could have belittled and ridiculed her husband. But she stood by and supported him even during that difficult time. She is a role model for all of us to follow.

Have you been supportive of your husband? I challenge you to allow yourself to become vulnerable. Let your husband know how important he is to you. Develop an attitude of gratitude in the smallest areas. I remember crossing a street with Frank one day. He stepped in front of me and held his arm out for me to stop until he made sure it was safe for me to proceed.

I said, "I really appreciate the way you look out for my safety—that I'm on your mind."

He looked at me with a puzzled expression on his face and I continued, "You know, Frank, I spent a great deal of our married life complaining about everything. From now on I'm going to tell you how much I appreciate you whenever the thought crosses my mind."

I dare you to try it. There may not be a noticeable change right away, because your husband will probably wonder what you're up to. But, ultimately, it will be like pouring water on a desert.

Submission

How do you feel when you hear the word "submission" in the context of marriage? Does it make you even more uncomfortable than "reverence"? The truth is, even if we don't like the thought of it, even if we don't understand it, even if we didn't realize at the beginning that marriage involves submission, as wives we are called to do it. And, believe it or not, it is a dynamic principle.

As an ex-atheist and ex-feminist, when I first encountered the subject of submission, it was repulsive to me. But I recognized that it was in the Word of God, and I believed that Jesus came so that I might have life and have it more abundantly. So I began to nag God for an explanation of this not-so-popular spiritual requirement. Fortunately His Word is true when it says to ask, seek, and knock. That's exactly what I did, and before long I got my answer.

God taught me that submission is a very positive, powerful, and aggressive principle designed by Him for every man and woman, single or married. It is positive because it was exemplified by our role model, Jesus Christ. When He walked the face of the earth He was an unmarried male, yet He lived a totally submissive life. He said that He always did what pleased the Father. In the Garden of Gethsemane Jesus prayed three times, "My Father, if it is possible, may this cup be taken from me"(Matthew 26:39). He pleaded with the Father to release Him from His obligation. He knew the pain that He would have to endure. Yet He ended His request with, "Yet not as I will, but as you will."

Had Jesus not submitted to death on the cross, none of us would have the gift of eternal life. So if we think salvation is God's number-one greatest gift, submission would have to be number two, because it ushered in our salvation.

Submission is also an aggressive principle because it requires wives to stand against the world, the flesh, and the devil. Those three voices attempt to convince us that, if we submit we will be subservient, inferior, and our husband's doormat. Nothing could be further from the truth! Our modern world teaches us that submission is a dirty word. No wonder Scripture teaches us: "Be not conformed to this world: but be ye transformed by the renewing of your mind" (Romans 12:2 KJV).

Submission is not a four-letter word. In fact, from God's perspective it incorporates four words: hope, help, holy, and freedom. When we hope in God's help it causes us to be holy and sets us free!

The principle of submission (yielding) should begin in single life and extend into marriage as we submit to God (James 4:7), our pastor (Hebrews 13:17), the government (1 Peter 2:13), and our employer (1 Peter 2:18).

After single men and women have exercised their submission muscles with those God-designated, final decision-makers, they are more prepared to enter marriage. The married man is called to submit to God in loving his wife as Christ loved the church—being the spiritual leader, being the final decision-maker, and living with her in understanding. The married woman is instructed to submit to her husbands final decisions, trusting that, ultimately, God will have the last word.

I compare submission to a broken traffic signal. When we come to a four-way busy intersection and the traffic signal is down what do we do? We should first stop to yield to the person on our right, taking turns as we pass through the intersection. What do you think would happen if that basic driving rule had never been instituted? Can you imagine the confusion with people entering the intersection demanding their right-of-way?

So it is with the principle of submission. It's clear that God knew He was creating independent, self-centered, and opinionated humans. This means He also knew that if we spent any amount of time with people on our jobs, in our church, or at home, sooner or later the signal of communication would go down.

If there were not an order of authority established, we would be in the middle of the intersection of our lives confused, angry, and demanding our own way. Unfortunately, because many Christians have not learned the power contained in the principle of submission they are suffering unnecessarily. As a judge once said, "Ignorance of the law does not excuse us from the penalty of the law."

So how does submission work? Remember, submission is first and foremost an attitude that recognizes God as the decision-maker. It is He who has established order in the home. When you don't agree with your husband, it's all right to talk about it until you find yourself becoming angry enough to sin through your words and actions. It's then that you must stop—leave the room if necessary—until you can speak the truth in agape love, with no strings attached. At this point, you are to allow your husband to make the final decision, remembering that God has the last word.

If your husband decides to go against the way you think, you are called to yield, to give it all up to God. This gives God the opportunity to show you what His will is in the situation. God will attempt to communicate with your husband, but if he chooses not to listen and makes a mistake, you then have the occasion to extend forgiveness and understanding and to allow God to fix the error. Meanwhile, your husband will remember why you didn't agree with the decision, and he'll be grateful that you are not saying, "I told you so." Those four words, by the way, only put him on the defensive.

Years after I began practicing the principle of submission in my marriage, Frank told me that when I began to submit to him, it put the fear of God in his heart. He knew that God was holding him accountable for the decisions he was making. His struggle was no longer with me but with the Lord. The reason submission is so powerful is because it operates on pure faith—the kind of faith that is "the substance of things hoped for, the evidence of things not seen" (Hebrews 11:1 KJV).

When I allow Frank to make the final decision and believe that God has the last word, it is my statement of faith that says, "I believe God sees all, knows all, and will intervene on my behalf." As I release the decision to the Lord, I then give Him the space to show me His will. And, by the way, "His will" doesn't mean knowing who was right and who was wrong. Sometimes we can have all the facts and still not understand God's will.

One thing we do know, however, is that God wills for us, as wives, to show respect—reverence—for our husbands. He wants us to be loyal to them, to be supportive—to be encouraging.

God calls the married woman to submit to her husband's final decisions. All these steps depend upon a sincere obedience to God's Word. They require humility and dependence on Him. And they promise us something that we cannot acquire through any other means: a marriage relationship that is rooted and grounded in God's love, fed by His Word, and fruitful through His blessings.

Points to Remember

- Many married women did not see their mothers exemplifying godly respect toward their husbands. Therefore, we must be committed to unlearn the incorrect teaching and educate ourselves on how to do it properly.

- God calls us to reverence our husbands.

- Even if a wife does not respect her husband, she must reverence his position.

- We should do everything in our power to be loyal to our husbands and protect their hearts and reputations.

- Encouragement and positive reinforcement supports our husbands and produces edification.

- Submission to our husbands' final decisions (which does not include anything immoral) is required by God whether we understand it or not. Fortunately, He has taken to the time to more than amply explain this powerful principle.

- A wife can help in her husband's development by being respectful, loyal, and supportive.

Assignment

1. Reflect on how your mother treated your father. In what ways has this influenced your attitudes and actions towards your husband?

2. If you were not raised with a father, think about where you learned how to treat and respond to your husband.

3. Study your actions and attitudes towards your husband. On a daily basis are you:

   a. respectful?

   b. reverent?

   c. loyal?

   d. supportive?

   e. submissive?

   If not, will you repent and commit to practicing these godly principles?

8

$\mathcal{M}$aking
Money Work

Bunny

Do you run out of money before you run out of month? Well, join the crowd. Most married couples face ongoing financial frustrations. It was years before Frank and I understood and began to implement God's principles regarding money. And, as Frank will soon report, this particular subject was excruciating for both of us to tackle. Many technical budget books are available to assist you in constructing a workable system for your family. However, by the end of this chapter, we hope you'll recognize the importance of 12 key principles:

1. Know the true source of your provisions.

2. Learn to live within your means.

3. Pay cash whenever possible.

4. Don't kite (anticipate availability of future funds).

5. Plan for the future.

6. Make Jesus—not money—your first love.

7. Know that a faithful man or woman will be richly blessed.

8. Be honest in your financial dealings.

9. Avoid fast money.

10. Become aware of what you treasure most.

11. Don't cosign loans for people.

12. Give regularly.

Frank

For several years Bunny and I had no formula for bringing our finances in line with God's Word. Money was one of our most difficult challenges. I felt I could do with or without a lot of money, but that particular attitude can sometimes cause you to make less-than-wise fiscal decisions.

It also took me a long time to realize that even though I married a wife who is brilliant in many areas, Bunny literally had no math logic. Before they created Readytellers (ATMs) and telephone services to check your daily balance, she thought the way to balance her checkbook was to close the account and open another one at a different bank! Together we were able to make quite a financial mess. But we were working towards our Master's degree, so we knew it was an area that had to be addressed.

As you probably know, one of the principle agitators in the destruction of marriages is money. I remember some irritating conversations Bunny and I used to have. She would say, "I will be so glad when we can fix up the house," or "Wouldn't it be great if we had more water pressure coming through our showers?" Sometimes during a rainstorm she might say, "We really need to get those leaks in the ceiling fixed before the water ruins the wood."

Now I could see the rain pouring through the roof like it was a sieve. In fact, I was running around with 12 pots in my hands, looking for anything I could find to catch the rain coming in. In my mind I was thinking, "If you want it fixed now, then you fix it—but please don't talk to me about it!"

It wasn't Bunny's fault. In each instance she was merely expressing a hope which my ego was powerless to entertain because, at the time, we were broke—or at least short on funds. The problem was, when money was tight I became irritated. And whenever Bunny would bring up the subject—or anything that required spending—she was jerking my chain and I was barking.

Bunny

Even though Frank was barking, I was oblivious to the negative effect my statements were having on him. Those needs weren't really that important to me, and the comments were simply consistent observations on my part. I couldn't understand why Frank became so upset when I would return from shopping and announce, "Guess what, Honey, I saved you 200 dollars today at a clothes sale!"

Frank would respond dryly, "OK, then give me the 200 dollars."

I've discovered, however, that Frank is not alone. God has placed an innate desire in a man's heart to provide for his family. And he feels less than adequate when he can't meet their needs and desires.

Some wives might say, "But my husband doesn't work to provide for the household." In some instances that is true. But that usually means that the natural instinct placed in his heart by God has been distorted in some way. All is not lost, however. As we've learned, a wife can turn any situation over to the Lord concerning her husband and allow God to fix him.

In going for our Master's degree in finances, we have to accept, once again, that men and women communicate and respond differently concerning financial planning and challenges.

Hopefully, what we have to say will help you and your spouse work through the money maze.

Money, Money, Money

Frank

I'm sure you have your own stories about how money has affected the environment in your home. In fact, money itself is not the problem. There is nothing wrong with money. The Bible only says that it is the *love* of money that's the root of all evil (1 Timothy 6:10). It sure was making a Frankenstein out of me.

Of course, some people say that it is the lack of money—not the love of it—that is the root of all evil. That is not the case, however, because the very pursuit of money can be enslaving. And the Bible clearly states that whoever seeks silver will never be satisfied: "Whoever loves money never has money enough; whoever loves wealth is never satisfied with his income" (Ecclesiastes 5:10).

That is why the 12 principles for making money work are vital. Money itself is good and important. Every society on earth has some form of money in its economic system. Ecclesiastes 10:19 rightly says that "money is the answer for everything." Money is necessary for buying food, shelter, transportation, clothing, and education for our children. You also need money for insurance and medical needs. On the other hand, our pastor always reminds us that "if your outgo exceeds your income then your upkeep will be your downfall!"

1. *Know the true source of your provisions.*

When you feel inundated with family responsibilities and financial pressures, always remember: God is your providing source. It is not your job or your employer. It is not even your spouse. If he or she is laid off from work or you and your wife feel strongly that she needs to stay at home and raise the children, pray about it. Don't get upset or worried. *Look to God as your source.* Paul states in Philippians 4:19 KJV, "My God [not anyone or anything else. He may use whatever He wishes as a conduit for getting His resources to you] shall supply all of your need according to his riches in glory by Christ Jesus."

2. *Learn to live within your means.*

So often it isn't our needs that we're worried about—it's our wants. And one of the things we want is status. You do know what status is, don't you? A simple definition is: When you buy things you can't afford to impress people you don't know and they don't care. It is an easy trap to fall into if you are not careful. Your neighbor gets a new car, therefore you want a new car. Your brother and his wife buy a motor home, therefore you and your wife want a motor home. Before you know it, you are stressed out with trying to keep up with the Joneses.

The Temptations used to sing a song entitled "Don't Let the Joneses Get You Down." Or, as Pastor Hill used to say, "If you can't run with the Joneses, the Smiths are all right." The point is, *learn to live within your own means,* and be content with God meeting your basic needs.

Paul warns us again when he says,

> Do not be anxious about anything, but in everything, by prayer and petition, with thanksgiving, present your requests to God. And the peace of God, which transcends all understanding, will guard your hearts [the seat of your will] and your minds [where decisions are weighed] in Christ Jesus (Philippians 4:6).

Paul goes on to say,

> "I have learned the secret of being content in any and every situation" (Philippians 4:12).

3. Pay cash whenever possible.

One of the ways in which we end up placing our future in hock is by living on borrowed money. "Charge it!" is said more often in America today than "hello." We have been living on credit for so long we don't identify with the concept of paying cash.

Today, American citizens constitute the most indebted nation in the world, and many of us don't remember how long it's been that way. Scripture suggests an alternative—that we should pay as we go. Listen to Proverbs 22:7: "The rich rule over the poor, and the borrower is a servant to the lender." Romans 13:8 is more direct. It says: "Let no debt remain outstanding, except the continuing debt to love one another."

When Bunny and I began to implement biblical financial principles, our goal was to become debt-free. We stopped using credit cards, except those that have to be paid off monthly. We also utilized layaway plans for major purchases. We made a decision we would *pay cash* for everything with rare exceptions. We have worked hard to keep that commitment. Before we developed that discipline, I hated going to the mailbox because it was full of bills (many with late charges). That no longer applies to us today, but it still holds true for several couples we know who have made the mistake of spending money they didn't have.

4. Don't kite.

Reggie, a bright young executive, landed a major account for his firm and collected for himself a hefty bonus. After closing two additional smaller deals, he felt he was on a roll and could, therefore, assume that his annual salary was going to be higher than before. He concluded this despite the fact that up until then cash flow had always been touch and go for him.

Reggie bought a brand-new car for himself, a brand new car for his wife, and a brand-new home to go with their brand new child. Less than two years later, the bottom fell out. He had to sell or lose everything because he was buying things on what he believed he was going to make. Reggie wasn't being honest with himself.

We all know people or have friends who casually write checks expecting money to come in to cover them. Often, moving funds from one account to another to try to stay one step ahead of the bank is practiced. Some people call this practice "kiting," and James 4:13,14 warns us against it:

> Now listen, you who say, "Today or tomorrow we will go to this or that city, spend a year there, carry on business and make money." Why, you do not even know what will happen tomorrow. What is your life? You are a mist that appears for a little while and then vanishes. Instead, you ought to say, "If it is the Lord's will, we will live and do this or that.

5. *Plan for the future.*

The subject of the unpredictability of the future has another side. Bunny often laments the fact that so many women are left to grieve the death of their spouse while sifting through a pile of unpaid bills, unmade wills, and no life insurance.

Bunny

I remember a time when Frank would answer the question, "Honey, is our life insurance up to date?" with "No, but God's going to give me notice before I die so I'll take care of it then."

Unfortunately, he really believed that to be true, and apparently he was not alone. I can think of only three husbands, now deceased, who took the time to plan for the future of their families before their deaths. How about you, husband? Would your wife know what to do, who to call, and where all the important documents are in case of your untimely death? Do you have a living trust or will the government get most of your assets because you failed to plan? Remember that a woman's greatest need is for security: mental, emotional, and financial. Besides, Proverbs says: "A good man leaves an inheritance to his children's children" (Proverbs 13:22).

Frank and I have a living trust and are continuing to update it. We have prepaid our burial plots and have a file set up with our pertinent information. If God calls us home together, our children will not be thrown into a state of confusion. The virtuous woman (Proverbs 31) could smile at the future because she planned and was prepared.

Planning for the future also involves wisdom in making purchases. Whatever "extravagant" investment you're thinking of making, you should first consider all relevant information.

"Is there anything wrong with us buying a Mercedes-Benz?" a married couple asked at one of our seminars.

"Absolutely not," I replied. "But before you do, please answer some questions.

- Do you have enough money to comfortably meet your monthly expenses?

- Do you have money in your savings or invested in insurance in case of disability?

- Are all your insurances—life, medical, hospitalization, fire, other disasters—up to date?

- If you became unemployed for three months, do you have enough saved to meet your monthly expenses?

- Are you saving for your children's education?

- Are you saving for your daughter's wedding?

- Are you saving for your retirement?

If you answered yes to all of the above, by all means buy the Mercedes or whatever else you're considering. If not, you may want to rethink the type of investment you're about to make."

6. *Make Jesus—not money—your first love.*

Frank

A few years ago I heard a song entitled, "I Work Hard for My Money." I suppose the real reason money is such a cruel taskmaster is because of what people will do in order to serve it. What do I mean when I say serve it? Some people lie, cheat, steal, and kill to get it. Some people will even sell their loved ones in order to acquire money! For them, enslavement to money is worse than being addicted to drugs. No wonder Jesus says,

> No one can serve two masters. Either he will hate the one and love the other, or he will be devoted to the one and despise the other. You cannot serve both God and money (Matthew 6:24).

In light of this, we need to reconsider our priorities. We have to stop and decide to make Jesus our first love, not money. Whenever a decision regarding finances arises, our trust in God and love of Jesus will dictate the course of our actions.

7. *Know that a faithful man or woman will be richly blessed.*

Our financial dealings must be honest and aboveboard. Take for instance Abraham's disposition towards selecting the land God was giving to him and his family. He allowed Lot, his nephew, to choose whatever land he wanted first. Abraham knew God was going to bless him due to his complete trust in Him, because he was faithful.

Abraham did not need to get stressed out over making sure he took the best land because he knew who he was serving and the one who had made the land. As Jesus said, "Seek ye first the kingdom of God and his righteousness; and all these things shall be added unto you" (Matthew 6:33 KJV).

Concentrate on obeying God (and that includes an honest tax return) and loving and serving Him, and He will return to you blessings for obedience. (Read Deuteronomy 28:1-10.) As Dr. Johnny Smith says, "If you will take care of God's business, He will take care of yours." The Lord will not go into partnership with a person who cheats or steals to get ahead financially. In order for God to bless us and our endeavors, we are admonished to be honest in our financial dealings.

8. *Be honest in your financial dealings.*

Several years ago, I received a telephone call from a friend who gave me some good news. This person had an associate who had hundreds of thousands of dollars and wanted to invest it in a music label. That sounded great to me because, as my friend knew, I had been praying for an investor to help capitalize my gospel music label.

I felt somewhat uneasy, however. I asked, "Where did the money come from?"

My friend explained that the investor had been a drug dealer, and now he wanted to straighten up his life. He felt because of the corruption throughout government and businesses in America, he had a right to keep the money he had earned illegally as long as he used it for good.

I thought, *Well, he's got a point.* And the Scripture that conveniently came to my mind was, "The wealth of the sinner is laid up for the just" (Proverbs 13:22). For me this possible investor was quite a temptation.

Not knowing specifically what the Bible has to say about something like this, I called a very close friend of ours, Gene Browning, in Alexandria, Virginia. I explained the situation and asked him, "Do you know of anything the Bible says explicitly about this?"

Without hesitation he replied, "Ill-gotten treasures are of no value" (Proverbs 10:2). After we prayed, I hung up the phone, then called and rejected the offer from the investor. And I am glad I did because God has been constantly blessing us. The old proverb is so true: "In the multitude of counsellors there is safety" (Proverbs 11:14 KJV).

9. *Avoid fast money.*

Scripture also states that "a faithful man will be richly blessed, but one eager to get rich will not go unpunished" (Proverbs 28:20). Suppose someone comes to you and says, "Have I got a deal for you—but you have to get on board right now, it isn't going to be available tomorrow! If you want to take advantage of this deal, you need to give me a check right now."

First, remember this: If God is going to bless you with a great deal, He is not going to rush you into signing something. If He has your name written on this blessing and you believe by faith this to be so, pray about it and take your time. "Try the spirit by the Spirit" if you are not certain. One way of doing this, along with praying about it, is to ask the person to let you see how much he or she is personally investing. If he or she can't or won't show you, it probably is not that good of a deal.

Also, remember there is no such thing as a free lunch. To say it another way, "There's a sucker born every minute." People who are looking for something for nothing are sitting ducks for pigeon-droppers and smooth rappers who promise them everything and then give no return. Chain letters stretch all across the world while low-flying helicopters peep into industrial warehouses at night searching for the latest pyramid scheme promoters. Lotto lines encircle city blocks while wishful dreamers lie awake around the clock waiting for their ships to come in.

If you are waiting for your ship to come in, be sure you have sent one out—through sacrifice, planning, and hard work. Those are the most dependable ways of creating security for yourself and your family.

10. *Become aware of what you treasure most.*

Colossians 3:2 advises us to "set your affection on things above, not on things on the earth" (KJV). Never allow your children to believe that any material thing is of greater importance and value to you than they are. If they accidentally break or ruin something, be careful that your reaction is not stronger than the love and acceptance you've previously demonstrated. Friends and family should never be allowed to feel that they aren't as precious as your material possessions. Things can be replaced—loved ones cannot.

Do you remember reading about the stock market crash of 1929? Many of those who lost great sums of money committed suicide. Everyday living is filled with so much uncertainty. No wonder Jesus instructed:

> Do not store up for yourselves treasures on earth, where moth and rust destroy, and where thieves break in and steal. But store up for yourselves treasures in heaven, where moth and rust do not destroy, and where thieves do not break in and steal. For where your treasure is, there your heart will be also (Matthew 6:19-21).

11. Don't cosign loans.

One principle that is consistently violated by Christians is the biblical prohibition against cosigning. What does the Bible say?

> A man lacking in judgment strikes hands in pledge and puts up security for his neighbor (Proverbs 17:18).

> My son, if you have put up security for your neighbor, if you have struck hands [which is like shaking hands on it] in pledge for another...go and humble yourself; press your plea with your neighbor! Allow no sleep to your eyes, no slumber to your eyelids. Free yourself, like a gazelle from the hand of the hunter, like a bird from the snare of the fowler (Proverbs 6:1,3-5).

Had I known this principle several years ago, I would have saved myself a negative blot on my credit record—as well as protecting a sum of money which I needed for my family. At the time, I thought I was merely lending my name and my good credit history to a friend.

I cosigned for a close relative who was buying a brand-new automobile. I should have checked the same credit history which the auto company representative checked—the one that caused him to require a cosigner. But I didn't. I signed. A few months later he became tardy in his car payments. Next he became delinquent. Finally, he had an accident in the car and stopped paying on the vehicle. It was repossessed, repaired, and resold by the auto company. Guess who had to pay for the difference? That's right, I did.

Remember, if God is our source then He expects us to be good stewards over what He gives us.

12. Give.

The Bible says: "A stingy man is eager to get rich and is unaware that poverty awaits him" (Proverbs 28:22). Meanwhile, the wise man knows that he should give to get, sow to reap, cast out to pull in: "He who sows sparingly will also reap sparingly, and he who sows bountifully will also reap bountifully" (2 Corinthians 9:6 NKJV).

God does not provide resources for us to become reservoirs of selfishness. He does it so we might become channels of blessings for others. Pastor Hill often said, "If God can get money through you, He will send it to you."

Bunny and I have endeavored to practice that principle while remaining open to the leading of God's spirit regarding what and who to bless financially. We have discovered that the more we give, the more God gives back. At first we didn't know we were practicing a universal biblical principle. But once you begin to put all the Scriptures together which talk about giving, you'll discover that God speaks about manifold blessing in return for your generosity. Take a look at Ecclesiastes 11:6 (NKJV):

> In the morning sow your seed, and in the evening do
> not withhold your hand; for you do not know which
> will prosper, either this or that, or whether both alike
> will be good.

"Good" in this context may refer to practical or economic benefits. Bunny and I were summoned by the Internal Revenue Service and told to bring with us our tax statements for four years. The red flag for them was the amount of money we were donating to our church and other charities from our income. After verifying our donations as true and legitimate expenditures, the IRS agent proceeded to give us helpful and pertinent information regarding ways to more excellently prepare our tax information and take deductions. They did us such a favor, and we were awestruck. Scripture says there is a seed time and a harvest time. The previous account was an instance of harvesting.

Tithes and offerings are instances of planting. God says to Israel,

> Bring ye all the tithes into the storehouse . . . and
> prove me now herewith, saith the LORD of hosts, if I
> will not open you the windows of heaven, and pour
> you out a blessing, that there shall not be room
> enough to receive it. And I will rebuke the devourer
> for your sakes, and he shall not destroy the fruits of
> your ground; neither shall your vine cast her fruit
> before the time in the field (Malachi 3:10,11 KJV).

There is so much God will do to prevent your having to spend money on things like doctor and attorney bills, accidents, or natural disasters. He will give you wisdom to stop any frivolous and wasteful spending habits. These are just a few of the ways in which God can rebuke the devourer for our sakes. This principle is summed up and merged together with principle number one, God is our source, in 2 Corinthians 9:10:

Now he who supplies seed to the sower and bread for food will also supply and increase your store of seed and will enlarge the harvest of your righteousness.

Do you remember the 12 principles we listed at the beginning of this chapter? Now that we've reviewed them, we hope you'll reflect on them and allow them to govern your finances. If it's necessary, they'll help you undo past mismanagement. They'll relieve the stress of the present. They'll also bring promise of better days to your future.

Assignment

1. Make the decision to become debt-free and chart a realistic course to reach your goal.

2. Cut up all your credit cards except those that have to be paid off in full monthly.

3. Ask God to give you wisdom and guidance in the handling of your finances.

9

$\mathcal{I}$n-Laws, Blended Families, and Friends

Bunny

Facing an enthusiastic audience, Frank and I were asked this question by Oprah Winfrey, "When you marry a person, are you marrying that person's family also?"

We had been invited as special guests to counsel a studio full of engaged couples. Our response was a qualified yes. A person's family is, by natural definition, a part of that person. Also, your friends and associates can be included as an important entity in your life. However, it is up to each prospective mate to make a decision regarding every other relationship that will be brought into the marriage. If two are ever to become "one," they must never allow anything or anyone to come between them.

It's often said that children from a previous marriage should be treated as though they were also part of the parent who is entering into a new marriage. However, children coming into a new family will someday leave and form their own family. Meanwhile, the parents are committed to being together until death. Although children from a previous marriage are ready to go into a new family structure, a common mistake is that they are rarely counseled regarding the roles, responsibilities, and relational abilities of each individual in the new unit. This is often a source of tension and misunderstanding. Not only are blended families a challenge, many couples are also confronted with the in-law (or, as some say, "outlaw") problem.

We've already discussed "oneness." Biblically, husbands and wives are supposed to leave their parents' family unit in order to start a family unit of their own. Although there may have been a period of time when both of them were single and on their own, they were still considered part of their primary family unit. Once they are married, however, they form their own independent primary unit—they become one with their spouse.

This is similar to the process of a mother who carries her child to term, feeding and caring for him or her by way of an attached umbilical cord. The moment that child is born, the umbilical cord is cut, making the infant an independent-though-still-interdependent being. That child now eats his or her own food, breathes his or her own air, and eliminates his or her own waste, independent of the mother.

God has created the family structure to evolve this way, too. Once a child is married, the umbilical cord of a dependent existence is cut. Unfortunately, many in-laws have a tough time with this because, in their minds, their child is still their "baby." But a baby that stays past his or her term connected to the mother can never develop and will eventually die. This is why a child is called an offspring. One day that child is intended to "spring off" into his or her own independent existence.

In-laws can pray for their married children and encourage and love them. But they must beware of attempts to reconnect the umbilical cord of dependence and, thus, tragically interfere with God's plan for the married couple's oneness—a oneness which characterizes His own relationship with His Bride, the church.

The Melting Pot

Frank

When a child enters into a new family, two things should be readily apparent. First he or she is loved and special and, second, everyone will have to make adjustments. Each household has specific rules which regulate the flow of activities and emotional cargo. These rules involve all sorts of things as varied as the use of the telephone, temper tantrums, and family devotions. Some of those in the new family unit will adapt more quickly than others. During this process, love's temperament called patience is an excellent garment for everyone to wear.

Inside our family room is a beautifully stocked and landscaped 90-gallon tropical fish aquarium. The fish are of all sizes, colors, and shapes. Each time I introduce new fish into it, the fish which are already inside the aquarium immediately stake out their turf. They communicate the degree of latitude and longitude which the new inhabitants will be allowed. Then gradually, as everyone becomes more familiar with each other, the barriers slowly disintegrate. And we are no different. What takes place in this instance is natural in the human family as well.

What Is Expected?

God desires to create families, but circumstances and self-will often conspire together, causing the destruction of one family unit and the creation of another. Nevertheless, we should understand God's original plan and what is expected of everyone. God's intent is that we should be "one." God's intent is that all are for one, and one is for all in the family. A healthy unit is a unit in which each member has regard for everyone else.

I take an herb which causes my immune system to multiply its defenses almost instantly. This multiplication of white cells causes a unique fortress which, in turn, insulates my body against the effects of germs. Germs which invade my body are instantly attacked by my defense system in order to preserve the health of my body. This same kind of unified front should be created when families (and in-laws and friends) are blended. Familial closeness should be constantly demonstrated both by word and deed: Within this home lives a single family unit, not two—but one—with a goal to ensure that every member feels special and loved.

Whenever this family unit is invaded by selfishness, rebelliousness, divisiveness, stubbornness, uncooperativeness, or any other unpleasantness, its defenses of love, unity, and firmness should merge together and kill the attackers.

The number one rule is that the husband and wife are the center of the home. They are not to allow anyone—not an in-law, friend, or child—to come between the two of them. Their oneness is the seed from which the entire plant of unity blossoms. Therefore, it is likely that they will be the first to come under attack.

Tactical Alert

Bunny

All attacks are not overt; some are covert, appearing quite innocent on the surface but very dangerous. These covert attacks may involve attempts by friends and in-laws to influence the decisions that are made in your house for your family. Always inform people who offer advice that you will discuss their ideas with your spouse and then, together, you will make a decision.

Like our tropical fish, when children from two different households become a blended family their tendency will be to stake out their individual turf and lay out a strategy which ensures them maximum freedom. With a firm hand, time, and love, gradually each child will become familiar with the other and barriers will slowly disintegrate. Each child is unique. Therefore, before the wedding, the future husband and wife should discuss together the temperaments of each child. At this time it is wise for them to develop a unified strategy for how each child will be handled.

Hopefully the husband and wife will love each other enough to recognize the inherent danger of allowing a blended family to be created without the necessary amount of counsel. Counsel needs to involve both the children and the parents in order to achieve a smooth transition.

Although it is not easy to create blended families that can adjust and succeed, just remember the incredible track record of children who have been adopted into families of strangers. Many times these children are aware that these are not their birth parents or brothers and sisters, yet the family's consistent willingness to go out of their way served to make them feel at home. This requires preparation and an environment where love feels safe and secure.

When we fail to properly prepare to follow God's pre-ordained goal for the marriage and family, dire consequences often result. Consider, for instance, the children of King David and his wives and how they ended their lives conspiring, plotting, and murdering one another. Think about how Isaac and Rebecca allowed Jacob and Esau to entice them into playing favorites only to end up with one son deceiving the other, while the other took an oath to hunt down and kill his brother.

The list of family calamities goes on and on until we realize that "God was in Christ, reconciling the world unto himself" (2 Corinthians 5:19). And then there is Christ also praying to His father "[I pray] that all of them may be one, Father, just as you are in me and I am in you (John 17:21). As long as the in-laws and friends adhere to God's structure for the family unit, His order is preserved and His plan of seeking a godly heritage is enhanced.

Let's Work It Out

In this chapter, we will be using interactive case studies to help focus on loving guidelines which will aid in the development of a healthy family structure. This format will also give you an opportunity to practice what you have learned in the preceding chapters. The principle goal of marriage is for two persons to become one in purpose, plans, and spirit.

Frank & Bunny

Case Study #1

Everyone at the celebration agreed that Ken and Marcy had a fairy-tale wedding. Everything about the garden nuptials, including the weather, was enchanting. Marcy's two teenage daughters were her bridesmaids; her 20-year-old son was Ken's best man. Marcy had been a widow for five years and Ken had never been married. Ken and Marcy moved into their new home after their wedding. Each daughter, Sharon and Priscilla, had her own beautifully decorated bedroom.

A month later, 15-year-old Sharon was watching television at 11 P.M. on a school night. Ken asked her to turn it off and get ready for bed. She ignored him and kept watching her program. Assuming that she had not heard him, he asked her again and received the same response. Shortly thereafter Ken shut off the television.

Sharon jumped to her feet, stormed out of the room, and shouted, "You're not my father. You have no right to tell me what to do!"

Hearing the commotion, Marcy entered just as Sharon exited the room leaving Ken exasperated.

1. How should Ken and Marcy have prepared the children prior to their marriage?

2. What do you think Marcy should do now that the incident has occurred?

3. How could Ken have approached this situation differently?

Our Answer

If Ken and Marcy had received premarital counseling with their children prior to marriage, Ken would have handled the situation differently, and Marcy's job would have been easier. She would be able to say to her daughter, "Sharon, Ken is not your father but, as you know, he is the head of this house and has the right to make final decisions. In the future I would appreciate you respecting me by respecting the choice I have made for my husband and the head of our home."

As in many cases, premarital counseling for the children probably did not take place. However, as Marcy strives to earn her Master's degree in marriage and remembers what she has thus far learned, we would recommend that she:

1. Remain calm. The sphere of influence with which God has graced the married woman will enable her to bring peace to this situation.

2. She should assure Ken that she will speak to Sharon concerning the situation and help her understand the order of the household.

3. If Sharon, while Marcy talks to her, storms off and slams her bedroom door, Marcy should be firm and take the time to explain what she has learned about God's principle of headship and leadership in the family. This would be an excellent time for Marcy to apologize if she has provided a poor example to Sharon in relation to submitting to God's family order with Ken.

4. Ken needs to realize that Sharon may be feeling rejected due to the loss of her own father (his not being in the home). Because she is only 15 years old, she is still getting in touch with her own emotions and needs affirmation far more than regulations. Ken and Marcy should setup a meeting with Sharon and allow her to express any reservations regarding her own sense of

160 — Majoring in Your Marriage

security. Afterwards, Ken should take the lead in expressing love for her mother (his wife) and his high regard for Sharon.

Case Study #2

Reggie and Delores have been married for 15 years. Reggie is a postal worker and an excellent cook. He would like to open his own restaurant. Delores's parents have offered to take out a second mortgage on their home in order to invest the money needed to open the restaurant. Reggie could make the payments directly to the bank. What should Reggie and Delores do?

Our Answer

It is imperative that Reggie not get so caught up in his dream that he loses sight of reality. If the restaurant does not succeed, could Reggie continue to make the payments on his in-laws' second mortgage? If not, and they also were not able to meet the mortgage payments, they would probably lose their house. If that happened, it might necessitate their moving in with Reggie and Delores. Perish the thought!

If owning a restaurant is Reggie's dream, it might be wiser to establish a savings course in order to accumulate the money or get a speculative investor or maybe a partner who is able to contribute half of the needed money.

It should also be noted that once Reggie's in-laws invest money into his project, they have the right to inquire about his financial situation and make suggestions on how money is distributed. It sounds like one big headache.

Case Study #3

Tim and Nancy graduated from college the same year. Tim is a financial consultant at a large investment company, and Nancy is a psychologist. A career opportunity has just opened up for Nancy in another state which would require them to move. Tim is currently enjoying success with his job and feels a move at this time would cripple his career. What should Tim and Nancy do?

Our Answer

The first thing Tim and Nancy need to do is pray and find an answer to the question, "Is God sending this opportunity along?" From a biblical perspective, the husband is called to provide for his family and to protect and promote their welfare.

Of course, if they had received premarital counseling, this area might have been discussed and decided upon prior to marriage. That would be ideal. However, if they are in this current situation without prior counseling and both want to go for their Master's degree in marriage, Nancy will have to trust God to speak to her husband if this is, in fact, God's will for their family.

If Tim is working towards his Master's degree in marriage, he needs to discuss the situation with Nancy and take his decision to the Lord in prayer and expectantly wait for a reply. Some may think that if he decides they should remain where they are it would be unfair to Nancy. That would only be the case if God were not in control.

While we remember that God opens doors that no man can shut and closes doors that no man can open (see Revelation 3:8), let's also bear in mind that promotion comes from the Lord. God may very well bless Nancy with a position in the city where they already reside—one that she had not even considered an option. Also, she may remain in the same position, but because of her faithfulness, in due season God will lift her up.

We could go on and on about the options that could present themselves. However, in order for God to bless the relationship, His established order should override any human decisions they could make. Truly, "we live by faith, not by sight" (2 Corinthians 5:7).

Case Study #4

John's mother, Vivian, had been living alone since the death of his father ten years earlier. Her health was beginning to fail and John's wife, Lucy, agreed that she should come and live with them.

Vivian ruled her own household with a firm hand and got very little opposition from John's father. He went along with whatever she decided. Not only was John under her authority for the first 18 years of his life, he has also adopted his father's, "Do what you think best, Honey" attitude with his wife.

Shortly after his mother moves in, she insists that everyone go to bed at 10 P.M. because that was the way she raised John. And, after all, he turned out to be a healthy and successful man. She also has difficulty sleeping when there is movement in the house. John and Lucy are accustomed to retiring for the evening after the 11 o'clock news. What do you suggest John and Lucy do?

Our Answer

After going for his Master's degree, John accepted his role as the final decision-maker of his home. Now he feels like a fish out of water. How will he ever stand up to his mother? Well, there is no time like the present.

1. We would encourage Lucy to have a heart of compassion for John and to be patient while he struggles with the situation (most men do that silently). Second, it is imperative that John meet with his mother concerning several issues. He should express his gratitude for all she has done in raising him. He should, however, be lovingly firm as he communicates to her the importance of being the head of his home according to God's Word.

2. After informing his mother of the family's normal pattern of retiring each evening, it might be helpful for him to suggest some alternatives (such as earplugs) when she goes to bed so she won't be disturbed by the movement in the house.

3. It is vital that John help his mother understand that he and Lucy make decisions jointly regarding the operations of the household.

Case Study #5

Arthur and Stacy have twin boys who are about to enter kindergarten. Arthur's parents are encouraging him to send the children to public school because they feel the children will be more socially rounded—just like Arthur.

Stacy's parents are offering to pay the tuition every year for the twins to attend private school to ensure their future college careers—just as they did with Stacy. Arthur and Stacy's parents have never gotten along, and they are anxiously awaiting the couple's decision. What do you suggest Arthur and Stacy do?

Our Answer

Arthur and Stacy should help their parents understand that their choice is not an either/or decision but a carefully selected plan based on the needs of their children. It's important that Arthur and Stacy communicate their concern that their children enjoy a loving and appreciative relationship with both sets of grandparents.

We suggest that the grandparents who would like to pay for their private education start a fund in the children's name until Arthur and Stacy make a decision regarding the children's educational future.

Arthur and Stacy should confer together before informing their parents of their decision.

Case Study #6

Harriet has been divorced for several years. She has a nine-year-old boy and a five-year-old girl. When Harriet married Jim, her ex-husband, Brian, made it clear that he would make the final decisions concerning his children. Now Brian telephones on a regular basis and tells the children they don't have to listen to Jim. What do you suggest Harriet and Jim do?

Our Answer

Wow, this is a tough one! Jim and Harriet, along with the children, need a very clear understanding regarding how the family structure is supposed to work. Harriet will also need to be firm with Brian concerning the guidelines for their family structure. Jim has the right to make the final decisions concerning the family. If the children are not willing to abide by that structure, other arrangements may need to be made concerning where they will reside.

Again, it is vitally important that these issues be worked out before the wedding! Harriet needs to understand that when she married Jim, according to God's Word, he became the head of the house. Since Harriet married first, then later came into an understanding about God's established order for her household, she needs to apologize to the children for the confusion that it has caused. She should also instruct them on God's family plan, and speak clearly to her exhusband about what will be allowed concerning her home and children.

Of course, this may initially cause problems but that is one of the consequences blended families face. There is no shortcut on how this can be handled. There is only one way: God's way. Harriet must do what is right—and leave the results to God.

Case Study #7

Janice and Pam have been best friends since the second grade. Pam was Janice's maid of honor at her wedding. She is still single and lives a block from Janice. Pam visits Janice frequently and is often there when Janice's husband, Phil, comes home from work. Janice tells Phil that Pam has been a stabilizing factor in her life for years—she would never interfere in Janice's and Phil's relationship. Janice enjoys Pam's company and would appreciate it if Phil would understand.

Phil likes Pam and doesn't want to hurt her or Janice's feelings. However, he would like to come home to his wife and nobody else. How should Phil handle this?

Our Answer

We suggest that Phil and Janice come to terms with God's plan for oneness in a marriage. We also want to see them become familiar with the obstacles which can prevent two people from experiencing God's best for them. Phil should make it clear to his wife that he is uncomfortable, he feels their relationship is being hampered, and he would like for her to resolve his dilemma by speaking with Pam. He appreciates the friendship the two of them have together, but feels that it crosses a boundary. He thinks Pam's constant presence violates the bonding that must take place between two people who are spending the rest of their lives together.

Once he has shared his thoughts, Janice needs to ask Pam to arrange her visits and phone calls to take place when Phil is not at home. Of course they can plan to do things together, but their get-togethers need to be organized around Phil's schedule. No matter what Janice's and Pam's response may be, Phil needs to be firm in his decision.

Assignment

1. Have you and/or your spouse decided to forsake all others and cleave only to each other? If not, will you make that decision today?

2. If you are in a blended family situation, clearly write down the expected guidelines for each child. Set a private meeting with each child and go over each point together. Allow her or him to ask questions. Try to answer each one calmly. Discuss the merits they will receive if the goals are accomplished and the demerits if they aren't (adjust this to the likes and dislikes of each child). Have the child sign the guideline sheet and post it on his of her bedroom wall. Finally, be consistent in following through.

3. Remember—only discuss your marriage with a trained Bible counselor.

10

Coming to Terms with God

Frank

After ten days of traversing scores of narrow roads and fast-paced freeways in central New Zealand, Bunny and I took a two-hour trip by air from Auckland to Blenheim, which is located on the northern end of South Island. Saini, a great friend of ours, met us at the airport and quickly drove us up into the mountains above the small town of Havelock on the Pelorus River. There we would spend the next eight days. She left her automobile with us so we could scurry about the rustic countryside for sightseeing.

Up until this time, I had never even considered driving during this trip because of my total unfamiliarity with the traffic patterns and steering design of automobiles in New Zealand—but Bunny and I were the only ones at the house. If we wanted to have lunch the following day, I would have to drive the car approximately 25 miles to the nearest town and back.

Bunny

Riding with Frank on that particular journey was the most uncomfortable feeling. The road was like any other road, the van was like any other van. But there was one big difference— Frank was driving on the "wrong" side of the road. Of course it was legal. Everyone in New Zealand drives on the left side of the highway, opposite to the United States where we drive on the right side.

Frank was hugging the center line of the narrow two-lane road, but I still felt sure we were about to hit the soft shoulder, causing the large van to spin of control. I forced myself to lift my eyes from the danger and focus on the rich, green-covered mountains and crystal-blue river.

It was interesting. I had felt completely at ease when a New Zealander drove us around during our first week on that beautiful island. The wrong-sidedness had been unique but not scary. But now Frank was driving. Yes, he has a good driving record but, in my opinion, he was out of his element.

Frank

When we started out on the two-lane highway, I kept repeating to myself, "Stay to the left, stay to the left." Just one lapse in my attention on this journey and it would be over, and so would our lives! Fortunately, as I drove towards town, traffic was light to moderate in both directions. I kept my eyes straight ahead. When I did finally check the rearview mirror, I saw a long line of cars trailing behind me, and a huge 18-wheeler was bearing down, encouraging me to speed up.

I was somewhat intimidated, but I remembered all too well another occasion in another country when I had attempted to drive 100 KPH, and had nearly lost control of the car on a deceptively sharp curve. With that in mind, I resisted the urge to panic and speed up. Not a minute too soon, Bunny and I arrived at our destination. Breathing a sigh of relief, we were able to enjoy a relaxed lunch in a small, local eatery.

As we relived our hair-raising journey, we began to see that it bore some interesting comparisons to marriage. When we marry, we must remember that arriving at our destination is the goal—not how fast we have to travel to get there. And, just like the white line which divides opposing traffic on a highway, what separates a marriage from success or failure is the line which divides worldly advice from the wisdom of the Bible. Our trust in God's Word enables us to come to terms with God.

Bunny

When we "come to terms with God," and begin applying His marriage principles, many things remain the same. We're married to the same spouse, probably live in the same dwelling, have the same job, same bills, and same friends. And if we have children, even they will be the same. But there is one big difference—God will be driving. Since His thoughts are not our thoughts and His ways are not our ways (see Isaiah 55:8), we may find ourselves traveling on the opposite side of our natural tendencies. How uncomfortable that feeling is!

It will probably seem like we're running off the side of logical explanations. The threat of spinning out of control may be ever-present, and the pressure from family or friends may make us feel like giving up or changing course. We have to remember to lift up our eyes to the hills instead of focusing on the dangers (see Psalm 121:1).

Frank

As we move along through our marriages, we cannot depend upon mom or dad or on our friends to transport us to the destination of marital bliss. We have to transport ourselves. God has shown us the road called "oneness," and He has given us the vehicle—His original plan for marriage—to take us there.

There is tremendous pressure from our modern society which is leaning on its horn, too much in a hurry to worry about the dangers which lurk around the deceptive curves. We need to remain cautious enough to know when our anxiety about the speed of our marital growth begins to endanger its very survival.

Bunny

One thing is sure: *God's driving record is excellent!* Even when an accident seems inevitable and you feel the impact of disappointment or doubt, He is totally capable of avoiding the tragedy. He alone can direct all things to work together for good. Not a minute too soon, He'll engineer life's course onto the road called "oneness." Only then are we able to relax in the knowledge of His grace and perfect will.

Checking Your Source

Frank

A traveler arrived in a city and inquired about reaching a particular destination from the airport. The clerk proceeded to instruct the traveler on how to reach the location. The traveler listened intently and said, "Thank you! But now can you show me that route on the map?" No doubt the traveler had learned from hard experience that one wrong word of advice can lead to one wrong turn resulting in going miles in the wrong direction.

When we learn from people—no matter how gifted or academically trained they might be—we are still learning a point of view. When friends and relatives attempt to give us advice regarding our marriage, it's important that we're confident enough in the Word of God to lay any advice alongside God's Word for comparison. The Bible is God's map to marital success.

Here's an example. Jack's father told him that the wife was created to serve the husband. So the young man has spent several frustrating years trying to convince his wife her sole purpose is to serve him. If Jack had checked the map, he would have learned that the Bible never states that the wife will be a servant *of* the husband. Rather, it says that the wife will be a benefit *to* the husband. First Corinthians 11:7 states: "But the woman is the glory of man." Something about the wife's attractiveness will cause others to admire and honor the husband—and this goes deeper than physical appearance.

Another example is found in Proverbs 31. A woman's husband is respected at the city gate where he takes his seat among the elders of the land. He is able to do so because of his wife's character, prudence, business developments, charitableness, wisdom, and knowledge. She watches over the affairs of the household and does not eat the bread of idleness. Her children arise and call her blessed; her husband also, and he praises her. She fears the Lord, her outward adorning is her inward beauty, strength, and dignity.

With all of this wealth which God has embodied in a woman, a husband should be careful to properly nurture her. If he doesn't, he makes her vulnerable to another man's advances a man who will appreciate her inner value and will steal her heart. Proverbs 30:21 says,

> Under three things the earth trembles, under four
> it cannot bear up: a servant who becomes king, a
> fool who is full of food, an unloved woman who is
> married....

If servanthood was the intended point in the biblical definition of marriage roles, Scripture more clearly designates the husband as the servant to the wife (I did not say the servant *of* the wife). The truth is that God calls both the husband and the wife to serve one another.

We certainly can learn much about the institution of marriage from others and their experiences. However Psalm 127:1 says, "Unless the LORD builds the house, its builders labor in vain." Many, like Jack, have attempted to build their marital relationship upon homespun philosophies or worldly wisdom.

Later they discover, often after several years of marriage—an infestation of underground termites which have slowly and insidiously gutted their relationship. Jesus reiterates the wisdom of the psalmist when He refers to a wise man who builds his house upon a rock. The rock of which He speaks is the Word of God. (See Matthew 7:24-27.)

Construction Begins

Of course, when we do decide to build our marriages God's way, we must be prepared to pay a higher cost since we are seeking the greatest return in value possible. We become like those in business who work hard—committing time and energy now in order to reap a far greater reward of wealth later on. Jesus asks, in Luke 14:28 (KJV), "For which of you, intending to build a tower, does not sit down first and count the cost, whether he has enough to finish it?"

Each winter along the Rose Parade route in Pasadena, thousands of people camp out on Colorado Boulevard overnight. Many of them start setting up their sleeping bags, tents and blankets, coolers, televisions, radios, heating lamps, and hot plates 24 hours in advance of the parade's starting time.

Yet there are many spectators who show up two hours before the parade is to commence. They murmur and complain. They even display hostility because they cannot find places or spaces in the front row in which to set up their seating area. Although they didn't pay the price by arriving early, enduring the cold night air, or experiencing the uncomfortable outdoor seating with the loud noises on the sidewalks, they are upset because they are unable to enjoy equal benefits.

As you are in the process of working through this material, you may meet individuals (including yourself?), who would love to sit in the front row as the parade of benefits of oneness passes through. In order to do that, you, too, will have to arrive early, not counting on a space to be there waiting just for you. You must go through the cold nights—and there may be more than one or two of them. However, you are smiling because you know that soon you will be able to enjoy the parade up close and personal.

Right now it would be wise for you to stop for a moment and ponder the cost of a successful marriage. If you discover that you are short of some of the necessary wherewithal, begin now to pray and ask God to help you. What are a few of the resources needed to successfully complete your Master's degree?

First and foremost, you need a supply of acceptance, forgiveness, and love. Believe it or not, all other items of necessity interface in one way or another with these three. You need to possess a love which is unconditional, an exceptional tolerance for your mate, and a forgiveness which is quick and liberating. Now I know that this concept goes against the grain of what is commonly considered reasonable. But these three virtues represent crucial pillars in erecting a successful marriage.

I said earlier that coming to terms with God requires stretching on our part. What did I mean? Look for a moment at what biblical marriage is: It is a commitment between two persons who will care for one another as they do themselves—thereby making them one. In order to pull this off, acceptance, forgiveness, and unconditional love are essential requirements.

Acceptance

What do I mean when I say acceptance? At the root of all marital self-image problems is the question, "Will I be accepted by my husband?" or "If my wife knew this or that about me, would I be accepted?"

"Wallflowers" stand off to the side while the parade of life passes them by because they don't believe they will be accepted. Many people are quiet and shy, not because they have nothing to say but because they believe what they have to say is too simple or uninteresting for common, everyday conversations. "Will I be clever enough, or informed enough or quick-witted enough to be accepted?"

Marriage assumes that acceptance of the spouse, including all of his or her flaws, will be a given. Bunny may not like all of my ways, but she has vowed to accept me—the person—to pray for my weaknesses and encourage me in my strengths. This makes it possible for me to lay down my excess baggage from the past and "be myself."

Criticisms from earlier relationships, along with the pain of rejection and ridicule, has already pushed many people into a shell from which they emerge only occasionally. One cannot grow while in a shell. And what does it take to draw us out? It is an environment in which we feel safe. A nonthreatening atmosphere allows us to relax, to be who we are without fear of rejection or put-down. It is an environment of acceptance.

Though Bunny and I had been married for six or seven years, I had never allowed her to see my feet. While growing up, I used to borrow my older brother's shoes squeezing my wide (size D) feet into his narrow size AAA shoes. After a few years of this, both my small toes grew crooked and pushed underneath the toes next to them. To make matters worse, my large toe nails are about a quarter of an inch thick. It seems like all the milk I drank as a youngster went straight into my toe nails.

Because of my embarrassment, I made it a practice to hide my feet by wearing socks all the time—even at the beach and around the swimming pool. After a bath or a shower, I would slip my socks on before I put on anything else. But through Bunny's consistent affirmations which communicated to me, "I love you, warts and all," I finally was able to expose my feet. For years now, I've no longer thought about hiding my feet because of feelings of inadequacy or shame.

This example may seem small and insignificant to you, but for me it was a challenge. What are you hiding? What about your spouse? Do you feel in certain instances that he or she is in a shell? If so, I hope you'll nurture an environment which communicates, "I love you just the way you are. I may not accept some of the things you do or all the habits you have, but

I will always accept you." This is what John means in 1 John 4:11 (KJV), "Beloved, if God so loved us, we ought also to love one another."

Turn the Other Cheek

This section does not apply to physical abuse.

As we learned in our communications chapter, one major reason for the disintegration of marital relationships is *verbal* bashing. While in the heat of battle, husbands and wives may move from verbally bashing each other to bashing one another's parents, then on to relatives and friends. Afterwards, so much venom has been spewed that only a miracle of God could bring complete emotional and psychological healing to that relationship. With that in mind, consider this: "Whoever slaps you on your right cheek, turn the other to him also" (Matthew 5:39 NKJV).

I used to love to watch the old western movies where a dashing young cowboy would ride in on a large white stallion, defending the rights of the poor helpless underclass. Sometimes, however, a young and inexperienced lad was easily goaded into a fight to the death by a sly and conniving schemer. And what did the schemer use to goad the young lad into a duel? An insult directed towards his lady or towards himself in the presence of his lady was all it took. What did the young lad give his life for? He gave his life in defense of his honor, pride, or ego. His life was never in any real danger until he fell victim to his emotions.

Jesus' words about "turning the other cheek" are revolutionary. He requires us to wait for His Spirit to lead us, rather than defend our honor. When you turn the other cheek, you're not in danger. As Paul states in Romans 12:19: "Do not take revenge, my friends, but leave room for God's wrath."

When our mates realize that we are relying upon God for our defense and advocacy, they will think twice before starting a fight. They will be aware that God will repay those who provoke evil. He reminds us not to be overcome by evil, but to overcome evil with good. Once we understand this principle, Satan is no longer able to use us or our spouses to goad each other into destructive actions.

Forgiveness

Of course, hurtful incidents happen. "How often should we forgive a person?" Peter asked Jesus. Jesus' response indicated that we should be as merciful towards others as we want God to be merciful to us. And history, as reflected in literature, indicates that unforgiveness leads to tragic behavior.

Due to his insane spirit of jealousy and unforgiveness, Herod the great had his beautiful wife Mariamne put into prison, where she eventually died. King Arthur had his wife Guinevere put on trial for adultery during which time his castle was attacked and he was mortally wounded. Othello was deceived into believing that his wife, Desdemona, was unfaithfully carrying on an affair with his trusted personal bodyguard. He plotted and attempted to assassinate his young bodyguard and then smothered his faithful wife to death. All these tragedies happened because of a spirit of unforgiveness.

Those who refuse to forgive a grievance are themselves victims of the debilitating effects of this disease called unforgiveness. Jesus says in Matthew 6:14:

> If you forgive men when they sin against you, your heavenly Father will also forgive you. But if you do not forgive men their sins, your Father will not forgive your sins.

He goes on to say, in Matthew 18:34,35:

> In anger his master turned him over to the jailers to be tortured, until he should pay back all he owed. This is

> how my heavenly Father will treat each of you unless
> you forgive your brother from your heart.

Can you think of anything more torturous than a perpetual migraine headache? What could be more agonizing than an acute internal pain the cause of which doctors cannot locate? What could be more frustrating than persistent fits of depression? These are the symptoms of a constant state of anger and bitterness. To refuse to forgive a person for a debt he or she cannot pay is to hold yourself in emotional bondage and place yourself under physical stress.

As long as I refuse to forgive, as long as I continue to require payment of a debt owed to me by someone who cannot pay, my fellowship with God is breached, the poisonous fumes of unforgiveness spreads, and I become a prisoner to my own emotions. This is like being under house arrest, because Jesus says neither will your heavenly Father forgive you if you do not forgive others. Now that is just too high a price to pay simply because I have been offended. I must get over it.

During that particular discourse, Jesus was teaching his disciples about life in the kingdom of heaven. First John 1:3,4 says, "our fellowship is with the Father and with his Son, Jesus Christ. We write this to make our joy complete." An unforgiving spirit creates a breach in fellowship with the Father and the Son, robbing a person of joy. John goes on to say, "If we claim to have fellowship with him yet walk in darkness, we lie and do not live by the truth" (verse 6). In other words, to deny this breach in fellowship with the Father and Son is to not deal with reality. We are only fooling ourselves; we are walking in sin.

But if we walk in the light of God, we have fellowship with one another and the blood of Jesus, His Son, purifies us from all sin. When fellowship with God is intact, His word continues to guide us while exposing unrighteousness in our lives. As we agree with God, and ask for His forgiveness, and forgive others, He forgives us and cleanses us. Then we move on to higher heights in Him, regaining our joy and experiencing greater dimensions of love for one another.

Divorce

I know that, as a Christian, God's grace is sufficient for me in every situation I find myself in. But I think we should take a look at what God's Word says about divorce. "I hate divorce, says the LORD God" (Malachi 2:16).

What are some of the other things God hates and finds detestable? God hates a liar, a murderer, a traitor, an evildoer, a deceiver, a person who causes dissension among brothers and a proud look; a look which says "It's *my* life!" (see Proverbs 6:16-19).

If you look closely at the above characteristics, you will discover that each one of them represents a breach of faith. And that's clearly what divorce is. Spouses have the right to believe that they have been told the truth; that their lives are safely entrusted to their mates, and that no plot is unfolding to physically or emotionally harm them. They need to be assured that what they are being shown is real and not false. Spouses should know that their friends are delighted to see them doing well and are pulling for them. To snatch this away from spouses is violence, and that's what divorce does.

Divorce is violence against the spouse and against the children. It is violence against an institution out of which the very fabric of our society is woven. Nor does it matter how we attempt to clothe divorce in respectability. God says, "I hate it!"

Little children who are faced with the departure of one parent cower emotionally in their mental closets, asking the same question Jesus asked His disciples after being abandoned by them: "You do not want to leave too, do you?" A child who has seen his family devastated through divorce lives with these questions: "Will I be left alone? Was it my fault?" Against a child, this is violence. Obviously there are exceptions, but you must settle within yourself whether those exceptions are acceptable to God:

When you make a vow to God, do not delay in fulfill-
ing it. He has no pleasure in fools; fulfill your vow. It
is better not to vow than to make a vow and not fulfill it (Ecclesiastics 5:4).

The marriage covenant we make with each other and God
is a promise which only love can be asked to fulfill. God will
forgive you if you divorce your spouse, but first examine the
quality of your commitment. Purpose to rededicate your marriage to God and work through the principles in this book.
And remember, the winds of change can alter every one of
your perceptions about your spouse except for the ones you see
through the eyes of love.

Love in Marriage

Marriage is the union of two persons bound by a covenant
and nurtured by love. Love is required in order for the two to
actually become one. How does this happen? Marriage is a process, and it takes time for any process to be completed. We
must understand that love has many faces—but only one of
them is enduring.

In the process of marriage, romance may, at various intervals, go on a lengthy hiatus but agape love must remain. There
may be times when one or both spouses feel that the other is
not a true friend, still agape love must remain true. Occasionally, sexual desire for a mate may wane and all but disappear for
a number of reasons; nevertheless, agape love must stand upon
the highest mountain, searching for paths which rekindle romance, foster friendship, and stroke the fire of sexual desire.

Recently, Geoffrey, a young professional whom I had not spoken to for quite some time, phoned me. While choking back his
emotions and almost at the point of tears, he confessed that after
15 years of marriage, he no longer loved his wife the way a wife
should be loved. He felt unappreciated, unloved himself, and
thought that, perhaps, he had made a mistake in the first place.

Geoffrey had done much soul-searching before he phoned me and had already dealt with the obvious issues of divorce. I would have wasted time talking about these. He had informed his wife and their small children how he felt, found an apartment, and moved out of their home.

His wife truly did love him, but because of poor preparation and advice regarding marriage, she had admittedly failed to communicate her feelings and her appreciation of his accomplishments. The Spirit of God led me to support him in his dilemma, but also to challenge him from God's Word. I reminded him that he was his family's covering, and for him to remove their covering was to expose his wife and children to Satan's emotional, spiritual, psychological, and, perhaps, even physical attack.

Additionally, I said, "You say you still love her, but not as a wife. Do you understand that according to 1 Peter 3:7, she is also your sister? Would you honestly leave your sister devastated, sorry for her mistakes with little or no opportunity to repent and escape such an awful penalty? If you cannot love her as your wife, can you love her as a fellow heir in Christ?"

His voiced quiet, he said, "Yes, I can," and he moved back in with his family. Geoffrey has found a new woman in his life. It is his wife. She is continuing to discover the wonder of God's love through the restoration of her home.

Coming to terms with God means coming to terms with His way of loving. Agape love teaches husbands and wives the value of romance, godly sex, strong families, and friends. The marital covenant is the binding agreement, but agape love is the glue.

Assignment

In your own words define:

1. Debtors:

2. Love:

3. Marriage:

4. Submit:

5. Friend:

6. Process in marriage:

7. Mature:

8. Patient:

9. Grace:

10. Pride:

11. Meek:

12. Faithful:

Read the following Scriptures (KJV) and note which one of the words above is within them.

James 4:7:

Genesis 4:3:

Ecclesiastes 7:8:

Proverbs 16:18:

Matthew 6:12:

Genesis 17:1:

Genesis 6:8:

Proverbs 10:12:

1 Peter 3:4; Numbers 12:3:

Hebrews 13:4:

Proverbs 11:13:

Proverbs 17:17:

11

$\mathcal{S}$ealed with a Covenant

⌐⁓⌐

Frank

The Pasadena Freeway is the oldest freeway in Southern California and probably the most dangerous. On one side of it is the Los Angeles River; on the other side are pockets of densely populated communities. It is a narrow, seven-mile conduit ending at the edge of South Pasadena.

Over the years, in an attempt to enlarge its capacity for vehicles traveling in each direction and to prevent further rush-hour gridlock, the California Transit Authorities have squeezed every possible inch out of both sides of the freeway and left very little space for an emergency pull out. Consequently, whenever a car stalls or an accident occurs, there is usually precious little time to respond, which results in numerous pile-ups.

On dry, sunny days, driving the Pasadena Freeway is usually not a problem if you stay alert and keep within the speed limit, especially when rounding the many curves. It seldom rains in Southern California but when it does, the water mixed with several months' build-up of automobile grease and oil leaks creates a time bomb for travelers. The slightest amount of precipitation turns the Pasadena Freeway into a well-waxed automobile skating rink.

My major concern has always been what to do in case of an emergency on some dark and rainy night. So, when weather conditions are good, I rehearse in my mind possible responses to various scenarios. Perhaps you have done the same in other circumstances. In case of a life-threatening scenario, fore-thought and mental preparation could make it possible for your family to survive.

In marriage, God expects us to conduct ourselves in the same way. As with any crisis, there is usually very little time to respond properly in the face of marriage-threatening assaults. Therefore, we must rehearse what to do ahead of time.

This, in fact, is why we have *The Covenant*. The road to mar-ital oneness is tight, and at times it is slippery due to the precipi-tation of stress and disappointments. The spirit of the covenant makes it clear that it is wise to consider ahead of time our response to difficult and trying circumstances. As with war and in business, one should always weigh the up-sides and the down-sides when planning for success. Marriages encounter a little of each.

Suppose you face irreconcilable differences or incompati-bilities? Suppose you simply fall out of love with your spouse or fall in love with someone else? What should you do? Let's look at the godly principles found in this statement from traditional marriage ceremonies:

> For better or worse, for richer for poorer, in sickness and in health, until death do us part…. I give you my word.

As we said before, marriage is nurtured through love and sealed with a covenant. A *contract* is made between people who do not trust each other. A *covenant* is made between per-sons who do. And the strength of a marriage covenant is in its three-pronged emphasis.

- First, the promises the two people make are to one another—*and* to God.

- Second, the term of the agreement lasts for as long as you both shall live.

- Third, we have God's blueprint for marriage to work out our marital difficulties. God's providence covers those who give Him their obedience. So He'll cover you—even if your spouse doesn't trust God.

Marriage is not to be entered into irreverently, lightly, or unadvisedly. That is to say, those considering marriage should get plenty of counsel. We know God keeps His word. Likewise, we are expected to keep ours. We are His children, indwelt by His Spirit, members of His family because of an agreement called the New Covenant. This New Covenant is based upon the sacrificially shed blood of Jesus Christ, and upon our faith in accepting Him as Savior. Evidence of our faith is seen through our obedience to His Word.

Obedience to His word is also evidence that we share His nature. First John 3:24 says, "Those who obey his commands live in him, and he in them." He wrote this to us—the children of the covenant.

When the marriage covenant is understood and abided by, our expectations are more realistic and our actions are more purposeful. The language of the covenant is expressed through statements such as: "I'll always be with you"; "I'll give my life for you; you can depend on me"; and "through thick and thin, with God's help, I will always stand by you." These are not the clauses of a contract. These are the promises of a covenant.

No Way Out

In a small Scottish town, a ritual is practiced which strongly symbolizes that society's commitment to marriage. After a wedding has taken place, the groom carries the bride over the threshold as they enter their new home for the very first time. Afterwards, the door through which they entered is nailed shut and is never used again. This signifies "In for Life," and a commitment to work through all problems which surface in the relationship.

This action is similar to the one taken by the explorer Hernando Cortés when he reached the new world. He ordered his men to burn all of their boats. His shipmates were very perplexed, and wanted to know why. They asked Cortés, "Sir, if we burn the boats, how are we going to get back home?" Cortés answered, "If we get back home, we'll get there in the enemy's boats." Obviously, Cortés and his men were motivated to win and, for them, losing was not an option. The marital covenant likewise motivates couples because losing in marriage is not an option, either.

When Bunny and I were first married, I believed she was a gift from God to me. That convinced me that our relationship was going to last forever. I knew that God's gifts were special; He had proved this to me so often before. Many times, when things were not going well in our marriage, I would reexamine my actions, my direction, and pray for guidance. I never once believed it wouldn't work out because I knew God would help me understand Bunny, His gift to me. After all, He knew her before I did—in fact, He made her. Yes, we would stay together.

The simplest and most visible symbols of the marriage covenant are the rings we wear. The gold signifies purity. The circle demonstrates eternity—that the duration of marriage is never-ending. The covenant points toward the fact that in the face of any adversity, whether in darkness or light, sunshine or rain, we will always remain together. Most couples can deal with the upside—the daylight and the sunshine. But what about the nighttime and the rain?

Can You Stand the Rain?

A few years ago I was in Houston, Texas visiting my mother. It was during the fall. The trees had a very rustic look about them as they began to shed their golden attire for the winter season.

Mother had taken in an old stray dog; she never gave him a name. All she called him was, "Here Boy." I noticed that the dog had developed quite an attachment and protectiveness towards my mother and her house. And something else stood out about this dog: He loved the rain. In the middle of a downpour, he would bark at the rain.

Well, on one particular day, as he relaxed in a shaded area of the backyard, a large tomcat jumped up onto the fence surrounding the backyard and set his sights upon a heavily stuffed trash can. Now, had he known my mother he could have saved himself plenty of trouble because mother doesn't throw away any leftovers; she refrigerates and eats them during the week. She has five ways to prepare yesterday's grits and no part of a chicken is thrown away—not even the feet!

Anyway, as that old cat spied out the lay of the land, he saw Here Boy laying in the shade. Immediately that cat humped his back, hissed in a low tone, and attempted to stare down his opponent as he came down off the fence near the trash cans. He circled the yard, and you could almost hear him thinking, *I'm smarter than you, I'm faster than you, and I can slap you before you can even say, "Bow wow!"*

About that time, a dark ominous cloud gathered overhead blocking out the sun. A meteorlike flash of lightning lit up the sky and a heavy peal of thunder shook the earth as drops of rain began to fall. The old dog seemed to look back at the cat and lazily respond, "Yeah, but can you stand the rain?"

Well, you know the end of the story: Cats hate to get wet; Here Boy won that round.

When it comes to marriage, adversity rains into our lives whether we like it or not. "Can you stand the rain?" It's an important question, because rain is inescapable.

Rain Is Inescapable

A major reason why many marriages fail is because couples have an unrealistic view of marriage. Marriage is two people, often with different backgrounds—sometimes from different regions; two people with different habits and perspectives and different languages who are pledged to become one. If you expect challenges and adversities to rain on your relationship, you will prepare to meet them. If you are not expecting it, a downpour may prove to be more than you can handle.

Adversity is the threshold of a crisis, but it also offers another option—opportunity. The Chinese character for crisis means "opportunity riding on the dangerous winds of adversity." The key word regarding a crisis is not adversity. *The key word is opportunity.*

When I was a child, after a heavy snowstorm Mother would ask us to go outside and fill large containers with snow. Rather than concentrating on the broken water pipes or blocked driveway, she would take that snow and make incredibly delicious ice cream. Looking back on my life, lessons like that have taught me that with every advent of adversity there also comes opportunity. Every time your marriage comes under attack, you can learn something which can help you grow.

A marriage will not always be sunshine and blue skies. Remain conscious of the fact that rain is inescapable. Therefore, change your outlook. Take a peek at Job's weather report: He says that "man born of woman is of few days and full of trouble" (Job 14:1). Although Job was a very wealthy man, he was clearly not exempt from adversity. In fact, it sounds as if there is only one qualification in life you need for running into trouble: You must be "born of a woman."

Jesus says that a house divided against itself cannot stand, and we know that problems can drive couples apart instead of bringing them closer together. The Bible reports that God causes the rain to fall on the good as well as the evil (see Matthew 5:45). Jesus also says, "In the world you will have tribulation" (John 16:33 NKJV). In short: Change your outlook—rain in inescapable. But peace is possible—even in the midst of the storm. In John 14:25, Jesus describes our source of peace:

> But the Counselor, the Holy Spirit, whom the Father will send in my name, will teach you all things and will remind you of everything I have said to you. Peace I leave with you; my peace I give you.

Peace is not the absence of adversity; it is the presence of the Lord in the midst of adversity. It is the assurance that He is steadfastly seated at the right hand of the Father, making intercession for all His children.

Many things can lead to adversity. Sometimes the man in the house is a poor leader, sometimes the woman will not let him lead. I have seen a prolonged illness or unemployment devastate a marriage. Innumerable challenges can create tension that causes tempers to flare. Whatever the circumstance, before you know it it is raining. Instead of pointing fingers at one another when it begins to rain, learn to turn your face towards the Lord and remember: Rain is inhabitable.

Rain Is Endurable

Rain requires preparation. When Bunny and I bought our house in California, the bank said it passed all inspections. The appraiser said it was fine, and the escrow company gave its approval. But that house could not stand rain—and we didn't know it until it rained. Then we had to put down buckets, pots, bowls, and jars. Afterwards, we tried on several occasions to patch different areas of the roof. We tried changing a few tiles here and there, but we never found out where the leaks were coming from so we had to eventually retile the entire roof.

Marriage is the same way. When we first got married, our friends believed that Bunny and I wouldn't have any trouble.

We were both successful, intelligent, reasonable people. The truth was, our marriage couldn't stand any rain at all. Satan knew where the leaks were so he conspired with circumstances—and we were not prepared. We tried little attitude adjustments here and there but nothing really helped. Finally we began the process of completely surrendering our old ways, our old responses, our old shells into which we would retreat after a fierce battle of angry words.

After we surrendered our lives (in the area of marriage) to God, we both began to see the source of leaks in our relationship. For instance, in my light conversations with Bunny, I started to notice her reaction if I criticized her ever so slightly. She would take off like a rocket, and I would be left wondering what in the world I had said. I had pushed her button without knowing it. But, with God's help, I observed different things she said sporadically. I learned more about Bunny the person. I discovered the reason she reacted so strongly after a small (I thought) criticism was because she had been criticized all her life and had little encouragement.

The Bible says that shepherds know the state of their own flock (see Proverbs 27:23). Up until then, I had been a poor shepherd. Now I try to be alert as often as possible. God said, "Frank, I want you to make up for all the times she has not been encouraged." That caused me to be less sensitive about my own fears of becoming too vulnerable and to look for opportunities to make uplifting comments. It has made an incredible difference in our relationship.

Bunny plugged some leaks in my life, too. She and the children used to accuse me of "always being right." And I thought, *How can a person who knows everything be wrong?* First, I seldom tried to see their point of view because I was too busy making sure they saw mine. Second, as I was growing up I can't remember hearing my mother, father, or other siblings say, "I'm sorry, I was wrong." Now that may not be a good excuse, but it was mine. Fortunately, with the help of the Holy Spirit and the light of God's Word shining brightly on my life, I found a golden opportunity for change.

Bunny and I, along with two of our daughters, 5-year-old Christy and 11-year-old Fawn, were riding to the market. Earlier that day during a tense exchange, Bunny had challenged me with, "Frank, I have never heard you say 'I'm sorry, I was wrong.'"

"Sure I have," I responded.

"When?" she asked.

"Lots of times," I replied, "but you don't expect me to remember little things like that, do you? Anyway, I'm sure I have."

Well, I probably hadn't. Because, for me, to say, "I'm sorry, I was wrong" would have been like skydiving from a 747 airplane. It was not even a subject fit for discussion. However, that day God had set me up. On the way to the market, Bunny and I had a disagreement. I said something I should not have said as I pulled into the market's parking lot and stormed out of the car.

The Holy Spirit whipped me mercilessly the entire time I was in the market. When I returned to the car, He said, "Tell her." With much sweat and under great duress, I finally succeeded in uttering these unutterable words which changed the life of my entire family: "Bunny, I was wrong for what I said and I'm sorry."

Believe me, when I said it I was relieved. Then Christy Joy, our bubbly five-year-old, chirped in with, "Gee, Dad, it takes a mighty big man to say he's wrong."

What I didn't know was that the night before, after I had clashed with Fawn over how she was handling her homework, she had told Bunny, "I'm never going to talk to Daddy about anything again! He always thinks he's right."

Bunny had disagreed, "That's not true, Fawn."

"Well," Fawn had retorted, "I've never heard him say he was wrong."

How grateful I am that I obeyed God in apologizing to Bunny in front of my two daughters. Only eternity can show the impact it had on them, especially on Fawn. That was simply a stronghold in my life. And Paul says in 2 Corinthians 10:4:

The weapons we fight with are not the weapons of the world. On the contrary, they have divine power to demolish strongholds. We demolish arguments and every pretension that sets itself up against the knowledge of God, and we take captive every thought to make it obedient to Christ.

So yes, rain is inescapable, but it is endurable. When we stay on the lookout and press through, we discover that rain has a purpose.

Rain Is Invaluable

Much growth takes place after the rain. Composer Andraé Crouch wrote, "Through it all, I've learned to trust in Jesus, I've learned to trust in God….I've learned to depend upon His word." Many marriages are much stronger because they have had to contend with adversity. So when you are being pressed on every side and you feel like quitting, don't look for the first, or even the second, way out. Look for the way *through*.

In the book of Exodus, after the children of Israel had been delivered from the bondage of Egypt, they found themselves trapped in a situation which looked more hopeless than the circumstances from which God had just rescued them. They started to murmur and complain to Moses, and he turned to God. God spoke to Moses and said, "Why are you talking to me? Go through!"

In obedience to God, they went forward and the Red Sea opened. If they had not gone through the Red Sea, they never would have reached the promised land. We must be willing to press through all of the storms in our lives in order to reap the reward of God's favor which has been promised to us—if we don't give up.

We are children of the covenant of God, sealed by the Holy Spirit eternally. We have God's Word, we have His Spirit and we have this hope: The marriage covenant will be blessed by God to benefit those couples who heed His Word. He will bless the marriage and heritage. Yes, the storms will come, but they will bring showers of blessing to those who choose to honor the covenant and find opportunity in every crisis.

Assignment

1. Review the three-pronged emphasis of the marriage covenant (p. 184-85). Then remember the vows of marriage you made with your spouse. Pray together that God will continue to strengthen your commitment to it.

2. List some of the "storms" you and your spouse have been through. Reflect on the lessons you have learned through them.

12

*G*raduation

Frank

I t was hot and muggy and, in fact, both the heat and the
humidity were climbing to an all-time high. Our alu-
minum seats were near the very top of the bleachers at the
south end of the stadium. There was not a cool breeze flowing
anywhere within the confines of the Rose Bowl, and even a
vivid imagination could not find a ripple of movement in the
contours of the American flag.

But down on the field where hundreds of excited students
were assembled, the heat was not the story. Today was the day
of their graduation. Bunny and I sat along with thousands of
other family members and friends of candidates who would
graduate on this day.

Launi, our eldest daughter, had focused her attention in
artistic areas rather than academia, and had dragged her feet
regarding certain requirements which were mandatory for
graduation. We were not certain if she would graduate at all.
That morning she had smiled and said to us, "Don't worry, I'm
going to make it. You just be there!" So there we were, sitting

and anticipating the sound of Launi's name to be broadcast as one of the graduating seniors.

Young kids were restlessly playing in the stands, drinking sodas, and eating popcorn while several of the parents chatted away concerning the rising crime in the neighborhoods and, of course, the heat wave.

Finally the school officials began the brief program. After the preliminary greetings, speeches, and entertainment, the list of graduating students was read. Each candidate paraded across the stage to receive his or her diploma to the sound of enthusiastic applause, especially coming from the section of the stand where family and friends were seated. Because Launi's last name began with a "W," Bunny and I had to wait through the presentation of certificates to over 1,000 graduating seniors from four different high schools. Even then, we weren't sure we would hear her name.

Beads of sweat gathered on our foreheads, and we sat on the edge of our seats as the district superintendent of schools neared the names that would include Launi's. When the sound of her name was broadcast across the stadium's loud speaker system, Bunny and I leapt to our feet letting out a loud, instantaneous shout, with many others in the stands giving her a salute. She'd made it, after all!

A Cloud of Witnesses

What about you and your quest for your Master's degree? Have you been willing to go to the degree of the Master— Jesus—in your marriage? Is your graduation day approaching? Have you taken care of the mandatory requirements or have you been dragging your feet?

Many younger couples and onlookers may be playing in the stands or drinking refreshments or looking for a place in the shade to escape the stifling heat of their struggles. Yet, seeing you graduate is the reason they are there. Watching you receive your Master's degree is the inspiration they may need to continue.

Why are so many other couples—who are in love with each other, watching you and your spouse? It is because the failure rate of marriages is so great, and they are desperate to find successful role models who will encourage them not to give up. They are looking for graduates like you and your spouse who in spite of the heat, the tests, and the trials, are still standing and waiting for their names to be called. They want to see you and your spouse receive your diploma! The writer of Hebrews challenges us:

> Since we are surrounded by such a great cloud of witnesses [those who have successfully matriculated and graduated], let us throw off everything that hinders and the sin that so easily entangles, and let us run with perseverance, the race marked out for us. Let us fix our eyes on Jesus, the author and perfecter of our faith (Hebrews 12:1,2).

Internship

Remember that graduation does not mean that you stop the process of marital growth and effort. When people acquire an earthly master's degree, they know that their degree only serves to help them obtain success in their future endeavors. Likewise, the principles contained in this book will need to be refined through the years of your own experiences in order to reap the full benefits of your commitment.

Following is a list of ongoing assignments which will take a minimum of three years to complete. Your internship will be concluded when all requirements are met and your Certificate of Completion has been signed by the proper authority—your spouse. In the event you are working through this material alone, you may obtain the official Certificate of Completion from the person you have permitted to hold you accountable for your commitment to these principles.

Daily

- Pray together.
- Have personal, private devotions.
- Compliment one another three times a day.

Weekly

- Practice communication exercises.
- Relieve your spouse of one of his or her daily responsibilities.
- Go out on a date.
- Share family devotions.

Monthly

- Discuss family expenses making sure to stay within the boundaries of your budgetary restrictions.
- Schedule special time with each child.

Semiannually

- Get away to review your goals and update them where necessary.
- Select an area in your character which needs development. Direct your attention to that area in prayer, Bible study, and the oversight of the Holy Spirit.

Annually

- Take a family vacation.

Challenges Along the Road

Bunny

The hidden cottage was nestled between surrounding mountains with vegetation so thick it looked like dark-green lamb's wool. Floating, billowy, white clouds rested among the towering pine trees. A cascading river flowed beneath our dwelling with water bubbling over rocks like a thousand twirling dancers. Flowers of every color and kind sealed the landscape with an artist's touch. The hills reverberated with a sound-track full of crickets, birds, bleating sheep, and mooing cows. Thoroughbred horses grazed at a distance. Surely this was heaven on earth!

Becky, a local resident, recommended that I hike to the top of the mountain so I could get a full view of the valley. Because of my love for walking, the idea was intriguing. I had never been one for nature walks in the United States because there seemed to be too many hidden dangers. However, New Zealand is the only country in the world with no venomous reptiles or insects. So, with that fear removed, I felt fully confident and stimulated to attempt the climb. My challenge was to get to the top.

Looking at the hillside, no path could be seen. Any ascent seemed impossible, insurmountable, impenetrable. However, I decided to start up the road, which continued to wind around the mountain. Stopping at one point before rounding a curve near the top and standing in the middle of the road, I closed my eyes in order to fully enjoy the many sounds encircling me. Along with the symphony of melodies came a low rumbling that seemed out of place with the sweet melodic vibrations of God's splendor.

As the rumbling grew louder I decided to move to the side of the road. At that moment an 18-wheeler hauling cut trees barrelled around the corner. Leaning flat against the mountain, the enormous vehicle passed within one foot of me. Dust swirled around and momentarily blinded my vision. Recovering from that near-death experience, I realized I had become so comfortable with what I believed could not hurt me, that I had failed to inquire about what could.

As you graduate remember to always be on guard. As you and your spouse apply the godly principles of oneness, many of the pitfalls and dangers to which you have become accustomed will begin to diminish and some will utterly fall away. But if you're not careful, just when you feel the most at ease, a truckful of troubling situations and emotional challenges may come barreling down upon you. As long as you're observant you can be prepared for whatever comes your way. But you must be on guard.

There was something else that caught my attention on that enchanting stroll. As I occasionally stopped and stood still to fully appreciate God's perfect sounds and splendor, before long I found myself swatting at worrisome flies or sidestepping pollen-seeking bumblebees. My moments of complete solace and comfort were constantly fleeting. Yes, even in this seemingly perfect place with the clean air, cool breeze, and comforting sun, it would never be perfect because of the irritating flies and bees.

Some people may think a Master's degree in marriage guarantees them a perfect relationship. Perfection can only be accomplished in heaven. The most we can hope for on earth is maturity. Just when you begin to admire the excellence of your marriage, you may find yourself constantly swatting negative thoughts and feelings (arranged for you by none other than Satan). And that same spouse who has the ability to carry sweet romance into the relationship also has the power to sting with unthoughtful words or gestures.

No, flies and bees we will always have with us. The most we can hope for is to put a screen (God's holy Scriptures) around our marriage to keep those pesky critters at a distance while we enjoy the breathtaking view of our oneness. Continually check the screen for holes that might allow those worrisome pests to penetrate your perimeter and invade your space.

You'll also remember that I could see no way up the side of the mountain, at least not with the visible eye. It was only when I began to move forward that the road came in view. Although I could not see around the corner, the path was there. As you consider climbing the rough side of your marriage it, too, may seem to be impossible, insurmountable, impenetrable. However, God's Word is a "lamp unto [our] feet, and a light unto [our] path." The road is there, and the goal of oneness is within reach as you scale Mount Marriage.

Finally, it was two days after my hike that I overheard a friend mention the danger of wasps in the area. "Dreadful things," she said, "quite aggressive. Our health board put out a printed alert concerning possible attacks." Why did she have to say that? First the flies, then the bees, and now the wasps! Every day exposed me to new fears. Pretty soon I would have to be content to sit and look out the bedroom window. But would that have made the wasps go away? If I ran from the possibility of being stung, wouldn't it rob me of hours and days of fun in this romantic valley? It seemed the wisest thing to do was to acquire a copy of the health alert, read up on how to avoid the dangers, and continue to enjoy my vacation.

Hopefully, we will continue to learn about our spouses. As they feel the freedom to be themselves, new situations—sometimes uncomfortable or potentially hurtful—will arise. Should you simply return to your old ways, secluded in your safe emotional closet? Or should you seek to know how to handle it? Let me challenge you not to pull back.

As the Bible often says, "It came to pass..." It didn't come to stay. Things have a way of working themselves out. Never let anything rob you of the joy of discovery. Continue to seek to learn more about your spouse.

Your Diploma

Frank & Bunny

Your diploma is found on the last page of this book following your final exam. You'll know when you've passed. The

Lord will confirm it and your spouse will reflect the accomplishment. Congratulations for completing this course. Now your "oneness" can be a witness.

Finals

1. Why should you commit a significant amount of time in going for your Master's degree in marriage?

   _____

   _____

2. What if your spouse has no desire to participate in this process?

   _____

   _____

3. How can we know we have placed our relationship in the hands of the Lord?

   _____

   _____

4. Marriage is not a romantic balcony, but a _____.

5. What keeps us from fighting the spiritual battle for our marriage properly?

   _____

   _____

6. Why should we attempt to figure out Satan's plan to destroy our marriage? What should be our response?

   _____

   _____

7. What are the five areas most vulnerable to attacks against marriage?

   _____

   _____

8. The greatest battles in our life are fought and won

   _____.

9. Communication is _____.

10. The Bible teaches powerful lessons on communication. What is the high point of each of these Scriptures? Proverbs 17:2; 18:16; 18:20-21; 25:11; Ephesians 4:29-30; James 3:5; Psalm 141:3; Matthew 12:36; Psalm 19:14.

   _____

   _____

11. What is the purpose of words?

   _____

   _____

12. Why are words so powerful?

   _____

   _____

13. Communication is the_____ of a relationship.

14. What is God's view of sex? (See Hebrews 13:14; Proverbs 5:18; 1 Corinthians 7:3-5.)

   _____

   _____

15. God meant the act of sex to be both_____and

   _____.

16. What is mutual satisfaction?

   _____

   _____

17. Sex is good. It is a celebration of God's creation. God enjoys it when we desire one another within the confines of marriage. List three reasons for having sex.

   _____

   _____

This

Certificate of Completion

is awarded to

_____

in recognition of faithful love, care, and
protection and a strong commitment
to honor God's purpose for marriage

_____

MAKING THE COMMITMENT TO A LASTING, GODLY MARRIAGE

The
Master's
Degree
in Successful
Marriage

EXCELLENCE IN MARRIAGE

Other Good ──── Harvest House Reading

KNIGHT IN SHINING ARMOR
by *P.B. Wilson*

A million and a half women will marry for the first time this year. But many others will become mired in a holding pattern, waiting for the right man to come in for a landing. This book breaks the holding pattern, showing women what to do while they wait, how to become complete in Christ as a single, and what to look for in a life partner.

LIBERATED THROUGH SUBMISSION
by *P.B. Wilson*

If you think this book is just for married women, you're in for a surprise. Submission, as it turns out, is for everyone, and destroys anger and rebellion while setting people free to love again.

SEVEN SECRETS WOMEN WANT TO KNOW
by *P.B. Wilson*

Using personal examples and thought-provoking illustrations, Bunny introduces women to the "S" factor—seven keys to overcoming discouragement, confusion, and frustration while soaring to new heights of joy and fulfillment.

GOD IS IN THE KITCHEN TOO
by *P.B. Wilson*

P.B. "Bunny" Wilson transforms the kitchen into a sanctuary of preparation, servanthood, fellowship, and communion. She shares creative ideas, family traditions, Scriptures, and encouraging stories to inspire even those who have never prepared a meal.

GOD IS IN THE BEDROOM TOO
by *P.B. Wilson*

Women will discover how to be mentally, physically, and spiritually prepared to experience God's gift of sex. They will see how to overcome temptations and accept God's forgiveness, healing, and restoration for past mistakes.

HARVEST HOUSE
PUBLISHERS